THE MURDAUGH MURDERS CASE

50 States of Crime:

NEW YORK: THE ALICE CRIMMINS CASE

CALIFORNIA: THE GOLDEN STATE KILLER CASE

OHIO: THE CLEVELAND JOHN DOE CASE

MISSISSIPPI: THE EMMETT TILL CASE

SOUTH CAROLINA: THE MURDAUGH MURDERS CASE

WASHINGTON, DC: THE CHANDRA LEVY CASE

THE MURDAUGH MURDERS CASE

ARTHUR CERF

TRANSLATED BY LYNN E. PALERMO

CRIME INK

CRIME INK
NEW YORK

THE MURDAUGH MURDERS CASE

Crime Ink
An Imprint of Penzler Publishers
58 Warren Street
New York, N.Y. 10007

Edited by Elsa Delachair and Stéphane Régy.

First Crime Ink edition

Cover design by Charles Perry, inspired by the French language edition cover design by Nicolas Caminade

Interior design by Maria Fernandez

Library of Congress Control Number: 2025935584

Paperback ISBN: 978-1-61316-694-9
eBook ISBN: 978-1-61316-695-6

10 9 8 7 6 5 4 3 2 1

Printed in the United States of America

"The past is never dead. It's not even past."

—William Faulkner

Contents

PART 1

A TRUE STORY IN THE YEAR 2021

1

LIKE ANY MONDAY

It was June 7, 2021. For several hours already, rocking chairs had been rocking, the air-conditioning running, mosquitos buzzing in the heat. Before long, the humidity would be suffocating. Alex Murdaugh finally dragged himself out of bed. At fifty-three years of age, he was not an early riser, and nobody was going to change that. These days, the bathroom scale read 265 pounds. That was a lot even for a tall, strapping man of 6'4". But nobody was going to change that either. After all, what other people liked about him was his honest plumpness, his amiable joviality, and his obvious good nature.

On that late spring morning, white strands mixed with the red hair in the mirror above his pink face. In this land of pine barrens and swamps of southern South

Carolina called "Lowcountry," Alex was a good ol' boy. Who would hold it against him if he slept in?

Alex slipped on his khaki pants, a short-sleeved polo shirt, and a pair of brown leather shoes. His wife, Maggie, had already left the house. Paul and Buster, his two sons, weren't home either. Only Blanca, the house-keeper, was around. All morning, she'd been busy in the big white house with a front porch. A little earlier, Maggie had texted, asking Blanca to stop by the super-market to pick up some pineapple Capri Sun juice for Alex. Actually, no, corrected a second message: orange. Blanca hadn't found any there but would keep an eye out. As her employer was leaving the house, Blanca stopped him. Not so fast. She looked him over, walked up to him, and reached up to his neck. His collar was crooked. There, that was better.

Alex Murdaugh climbed into his car, guided his Chevrolet Suburban down the unpaved lane between two rows of trees, drove past a low red-brick wall, and exited the estate, an immense, isolated property strad-dling two counties and surrounded by a gray-green-brown scrub–4147 Moselle Road, known as "Moselle." It was past noon. The shoulder was littered with road-kill, and turkey vultures glided overhead like they had nowhere to go. The roadside was a landscape of conifers, mobile homes, small Baptist churches, fast food restaurants, and gas stations.

Twenty minutes later, he reached Hampton, a burg of some three thousand souls organized around a few simple virtues. It had a main street, a few clothing shops, an old movie theater, and a coffee shop. And Coconut's, a restaurant with brown carpeting and plastic chairs, where the locals gathered over a plate of shrimp and grits.

Alex parked his Suburban a little farther on, in the parking lot of a large red-brick, neocolonial building. Called the PMPED for Peters, Murdaugh, Parker, Eltzroth, and Detrick, PA, it housed the law firm founded by Alex's great-grandfather back in 1910. Alex Murdaugh felt at home here. He was the most recent heir in a lineage of emeritus prosecutors. For a century, the Murdaughs had embodied law and order in Hampton County.

In the small courthouse dating from 1878 a little farther down the street, his ancestors' portraits hung on the walls: Randolph I, Randolph II, and Randolph III. Alex's older brother also worked in the family business. His name was Randolph IV, but everyone called him Randy.

A stack of papers was waiting for Alex in his office. His work as an attorney consisted mainly of defending good people who'd been victims of car accidents, work accidents, and health-care accidents. In people's most desperate moments, Murdaugh assured them, "I'm here." That's what he told his clients. He made a pretty good living—$125,000 per year, not counting the bonus.

Maybe that's also why nobody found fault with Alex Murdaugh's habit of arriving at the office so late. It had even become a running joke. Sometimes, he'd arrive at five o'clock, right when everyone else was ready to go home. And he did it openly; discretion was not in his tool kit. Annette, his paralegal, called him "The Tasmanian Devil" because he blew into the office like a thundering tornado with his phone pressed to his ear.

Late that morning, Jeanne, the firm's CFO, was looking for him. When she saw him upstairs, standing outside his office, she called out to him. What happened next was remarkable, only the first in a day that would include several unusual events. Alex Murdaugh responded with a dark look, which was not at all like him, and asked, "What do you need now?"

Strictly speaking, the matter wasn't urgent, but they would need to sit down for a moment to talk about money. He assured her that everything was in order. Or everything would be real soon. In any case, no need to worry.

The telephone rang. Sorry, he had to take this call. It was news concerning his father. Bad news. He was in the hospital and wasn't going to last long. Alex Murdaugh was not in the mood to discuss anything else. End of discussion.

It was about 6:30 p.m. when he left the office and returned to Moselle. The next to arrive was his beloved son Paul. At age twenty-two, he was a little hotheaded and loved the great outdoors. Alex's wife, Maggie, would arrive a little later. She was fifty-two years old. Alex sent her a text. "Paul told me you were getting a pedicure! Call me when you're done." While waiting, father and son drove around the estate. It was a gray-green paradise of over seventeen hundred acres that stretched to the horizon, with a small lake and trees rising into the sky. It even had a short landing strip for airplanes. To get around the property, the Murdaughs owned a fleet of golf carts, pickup trucks, and gardening vehicles.

Three hundred yards from the house lay the kennel where the Murdaughs kept their lucky Labradors Bubba, Bourbon, and Grady. An adjoining shed held some twenty firearms, including pump rifles, semiautomatic rifles, and .12-gauge shotguns. The Murdaughs had all kinds of rifles at the house. In many other places, this would have seemed strange, but who didn't own guns around there with so much wildlife?

That evening, they needed to check on the sunflowers and start organizing the hunt planned for the following weekend. Alex tried to stand a bush up straight, but it kept flopping over. Laughing, Paul filmed a video of him. In the glow of the setting sun, Alex and his son were having a good time.

Maggie parked her Mercedes on the property at around 8:00 p.m. Husband and wife had met in college, and together, they'd endured life's trials. Maggie had spent the day at their beach house in Edisto getting ready for the Fourth of July party. Alex had asked her if she could come home. Since she didn't like leaving him alone during this difficult time, she decided to join him for an evening with the family. Such moments were precious.

The previous evening, they'd gone to another baseball game in Columbia, two hours away. A week before that, they'd celebrated Alex's birthday. Paul had brought in a huge cake with white icing. While everyone sang "Happy Birthday" Alex blew out the candles and raised his glass, shouting, "Thank y'all so much!"

Before leaving, Blanca made dinner: cube steaks with gravy, green beans, and white rice. Paul loved her cooking. Maggie served up Alex's plate. As usual, they ate dinner together in front of the television, each in their usual spot: Alex on the sofa, Maggie seated in front of a dinner tray, and Paul in the recliner. Paul was the first to finish eating and went off to do his thing. That evening, he had to take care of Cash, his friend Rogan's Labrador.

At around 8:45 p.m., Paul and his mother went out to the kennel. Alex still needed to make a run to Almeda, twenty minutes away, to visit his mother, who was in the late stages of Alzheimer's disease. Since the kennels were some three hundred yards from the Murdaugh house, Alex texted Maggie to let her know he was leaving, then set out for his mother's house. On the way, Alex called his older son, Buster. Then he called his best friend, Chris Wilson, to catch up on his news. He also called his younger brother, John Marvin, who was watching a movie with the family. He said he'd call Alex back tomorrow.

Fifteen minutes later, Alex arrived at his parents' house. For a few minutes, he watched a game show on television with his mother, then left for Moselle at 9:43 p.m. He called Maggie, who didn't answer. At 9:47 p.m., he sent her a text: "Call me, Honey." It remained unread.

By 10:00 p.m., Alex was back home. There was no one in the house. Maggie was still not answering. At 10:05 p.m., Alex jumped back in the car and drove down to the kennel.

At 10:06 p.m., he dialed 911. In a voice struck with sudden horror, he shouted, "This is Alex Murdaugh, 4147 Moselle Road. Come quickly, my wife and child have been shot bad!"

In the chaos, the operator tried to understand.

"Did they shoot each other?"

"No!"

"Are they breathing?"

"No, ma'am!"

"Did you say that they are your wife and your son?"

"My wife and my son," he repeated, alone, facing the slaughter.

Sergeant Daniel Greene was the first police officer on the scene. The low brick wall, the lane that led to the deserted house, the crickets chirping—such a setting made everything seem diabolical. The young police officer switched on his flashlight and headed down the path that led to the kennel area. He walked past the only witnesses on the scene, the Labradors who were whining and barking in their cages.

To the left, in front of the door to a small feed supply shed, a young man lay in a pool of blood. A little beyond him to the right lay the body of a woman face down in the dirt. In the center of the shadows, the beam of his flashlight fell on a man in a white T-shirt and khaki shorts, his face frozen in a wild-eyed grimace. Alex Murdaugh. Eighteen minutes had passed since his call.

A hunting rifle leaned against the Chevrolet Suburban, which still had its emergency flashers going. Alex said that he'd gone to get a gun for protection, just in case. His voice rang with hysteria. He paced, crossed his arms, leaned over, putting his hands on his thighs—he could not stand still. Who could? He had checked the victims for a pulse, he said. It didn't look good.

"It's a long story," he added, unprompted. "My son was involved in a boat accident a few months ago. He received threats."

A few seconds later, he asked if it was official that his wife and son were dead. "Looks like it," replied the sergeant, his tone impersonal. He was almost surprised to have to state the obvious. Murdaugh's face twisted. He started to collapse, then managed to straighten himself up. He blew out a breath, sniffled, cleared his throat several times, and mopped his face with his T-shirt.

"Sorry," he said, as though trying to pull himself together. "I'm really sorry." Another police officer walked into the beam of the flashlight. In a polite reflex, Murdaugh asked him the most normal question imaginable. "How ya doin'?"

Where to begin? The police covered the bodies and secured the perimeter. McDowell, the assistant, found a cartridge on the ground and marked its position with a hunk of yellow police tape, setting a rock on top so it wouldn't blow away. Then they called their colleagues in the South Carolina Law Enforcement Division. Known as SLED, this was the equivalent of the state criminal investigation unit.

They established the following facts: The body of Maggie, fifty-two years of age, had been torn apart by the bullets. She had been shot four or five times with an assault rifle in the legs, chest, and head. Paul, twenty-two years of age, had been shot with a .12-gauge hunting rifle. The first shot hit him in the chest, and the second, even more horrifyingly, in the head. The forensic pathologist, who specialized in crime scenes, would report that Paul's skull had exploded and his brain had flown into the air before dropping at his feet. His face was gone. There was no trace of the two weapons.

At 1:00 a.m., Alex Murdaugh was interrogated inside Agent David Owen's squad car. The police officers were sorry, but they had to ask a few questions. It was procedure.

"I understand," replied Murdaugh, compliant. "I totally understand."

Between fearful whimpers, Murdaugh said that he had tried to turn Paul's body over.

"Did you touch Maggie?"

"I did touch her. I touched both of them. I tried to take their pulse. Then I immediately called 911." How was his relationship with Maggie? Wonderful. And with Paul? Also wonderful. So, who might have been angry at them? Alex Murdaugh had his pet idea, which he quickly served up to the officers and would continue repeating. Two years earlier, his son had been involved in a boat accident that resulted in the death of a young woman. The incident had created a scandal in the region.

Special Agent Owen was wary and told Murdaugh that the police would probably have many more questions to ask him. Alex, the devastated father in the passenger seat, patted his thighs as if concluding a meeting with a client. "I'm available, you know you let me know. . . ."

That would be all for that day.

2

THE CURSE OF HAMPTON COUNTY

Soon, other bodies surfaced in the wake of these two.

The first dated back to 2015. On July 8, a little before four o'clock in the morning, a tow-truck driver was on his way to work. He was driving through Hampton County at night, passing through an isolated area at an hour when it would be surreal to come across a living soul. Then he spotted some kind of obstacle on the road. Probably the carcass of an animal that had chosen the wrong moment to cross the road, he thought. But that's not what it was. His headlights revealed a horrifying sight. He called the police, telling them that he'd seen "a white man sprawled on the road." Then he continued on his way.

A few minutes later, the police arrived. A body lay stretched out in the road. A young man who looked frail, with a fair complexion. He was wearing a Nike T-shirt, beige cargo shorts, and black sneakers. The blood flowing from a wound above his right eye had discolored his blond hair and was forming a dark pool on the asphalt. His soft face was disfigured. The officers secured the perimeter, drew a red square around the victim on the pavement, and identified him. Stephen Smith, a student, nineteen years of age.

The body was taken away for an autopsy, to be examined by the forensic pathologist. The skull had sustained a fracture on the right side, and a long tear started at the forehead. The right shoulder was dislocated and the arms were covered with cuts. Cause of death: blunt force trauma to the skull. It was a hit-and-run, resulting in the death of a pedestrian, the report concluded. The victim was lying right in the middle of the road, so logically, it had to be a hit-and-run.

Yet the South Carolina Highway Patrol investigators were skeptical. They knew the signs that indicated a traffic accident, but the scene before them did not fit that scenario. If Stephen Smith had been struck by a vehicle traveling at fifty-five miles an hour, several things would have happened.

His body would have flown into the air, rolled, and bounced on the pavement several times before sprawling like a disjointed marionette. The series of blows to his body would have sent his shoes flying. His telephone would have been thrown from his pocket, and the impact would have cracked its screen. Friction from his body sliding across the pavement would have ripped up his clothes and torn into his flesh. In addition to skull fractures, he would have suffered injuries to his torso and legs. The impact of the vehicle would have left cuts and contusions on his body. This level of impact would have left scattered shards of glass and flecks of paint on the road, as well as skid marks.

Yet the road was clean. Not a trace of any collision in the area. The investigators wondered if the body had been deposited in the middle of the road.

Other details attracted their attention. The victim's car, a little yellow Chevrolet, was found parked at the side of a road three miles from the scene. The battery was still charged, but when the officer turned on the ignition, the vehicle wouldn't start. The gas cap, unscrewed, was dangling against the side of the car. The victim's wallet was still inside the car, wedged between the passenger seat and the door. This set off a whole new set of questions. If Stephen Smith had gone off in search of gas, why leave his wallet in the car? Was the gas tank empty, or had someone emptied it? And even if the young man had started walking along that road, why head in the opposite direction from the nearest gas station?

Another scenario began to take shape. This was not an accident. It was murder.

For Stephen's funeral, his family decided on an open coffin to let everyone see his sweet, mutilated face. His mother, Sandy, was convinced that her son had been the victim of a hate crime, and a year later, she would contact the FBI. Stephen Smith had been openly gay in a conservative area where being different was never a good idea. Furthermore, she knew her son, and he would never have ventured out on a country road all alone—certainly not in the dead of night and certainly not without notifying anyone.

His twin sister, Stephanie, confirmed that he'd been secretive in the weeks leading up to his death. Stephen had confided to close friends that he was going out with a high-profile resident of Hampton County, but he was evasive about that person's identity. His lover was still in the closet, and news of his sexual orientation would rock the county, Stephen had said.

Their investigation put the police on the trail of the Murdaugh family. On the day of the accident, a lawyer had telephoned Stephen Smith's father. Alex Murdaugh's older brother, Randy, had offered his services pro bono.

That was strange. A few months later, a man contacted the investigators with a tip he'd received from Randy Murdaugh. Allegedly, Stephen Smith had been hit by a car driven by a teenager who lived in the county.

Another name kept cropping up, and that was Buster, Alex Murdaugh's older son. Buster and Stephen had known each other since childhood. They'd been in the same class and played on the same baseball team, which was coached by the Murdaughs.

Rumors started circulating. People whispered that the two boys had been in a secret relationship, things had gone wrong between them, and Stephen had been beaten to death with a baseball bat. People said that the Murdaugh boys, Paul and Buster, had been involved. These rumors fed other rumors, and soon, people were saying other things. No one would speak out publicly for fear of reprisal. Supposedly, some people had been paid off to stay out of town until the whole thing blew over. Others had unplugged their phones to avoid having to answer to investigators. In all, the name Murdaugh appeared in the file some forty times.

On June 22, 2021, two weeks after the murders of Maggie and Paul, investigators decided to reopen the investigation into the death of Stephen Smith. The rumor was tenacious and the media would spread it like a virus.

The second body dated back to 2018. This one was Miss Gloria. At around 9:30 a.m. on February 2 of that year, Maggie Murdaugh called 911 from the Moselle property. Their housekeeper, Gloria Satterfield, fifty-seven years of age, had just fallen on the brick steps that led up to the front door of the house. She was still conscious but no longer responsive, so please come quickly! Paul took the telephone from her, and the operator asked, "Can you ask what kind of pain she's having?"

"Ma'am, she can't talk, she has cracked her head . . . there's blood on the concrete, and she's bleeding from her left ear."

The 911 operator asked if the victim had a history of heart problems, and Paul grew annoyed. "Ma'am, could you stop asking all these questions?"

Sixteen minutes later, an ambulance collected Gloria Satterfield and took her away. Circumstances surrounding the fall were murky. Maggie said she'd heard noise, had found the woman, and called for help immediately. Paul said that when he'd tried to help her up, she'd fallen again. Arriving home shortly after the accident, Alex maintained that the victim told him the dogs had made her lose her balance on the steps. But at the hospital, Miss Gloria was no longer able to explain how she'd fallen. She had several broken ribs and suffered a subdural hematoma from the impact to the skull. On February 26, three weeks after her fall, Gloria Satterfield died of complications from her injuries.

Gloria Satterfield had been working for the Murdaughs for twenty-four years. She had watched Paul and Buster grow up. She was part of the family. After the funeral, Alex Murdaugh visited her two sons, Brian and Michael (who went by Tony). Promising to take care of them, Alex made them an offer they couldn't refuse. The accident had taken place at his Moselle property, so all they had to do was sue him for wrongful death and wait for payment from his homeowner's insurance company. A payment which they never saw.

Years later, Gloria Satterfield's sons would learn that Alex Murdaugh had pocketed more than $4 million that should have gone to them. All that would have gone unnoticed had it not been for the boating accident. When a third body surfaced.

❖

The boat tragedy took place in 2019. Late in the night of February 23–24, a motorboat was cruising up a local creek. On board were six friends who'd known one another forever. Maggie and Alex's younger son, Paul Murdaugh, was part of the group. At 2:20 a.m., the boat collided with a piling on the Archers Creek Bridge. The impact split the hull, hurling three passengers into the icy water. One of them did not come back up to the surface. Connor Cook, who had broken his jaw in the accident, called 911. "Please, send someone." Behind him, horrified voices were screaming out to the sixth passenger, who had not reappeared. It was Mallory Beach, nineteen years of age.

Emergency services arrived on the bridge. The damaged boat belonged to the Murdaugh family. Paul asked the police if he could borrow their phone. He just wanted to notify his grandfather. He smiled. His friend Anthony Cook, who was Connor's cousin, leaped up and started shouting at him, "You fucking smiling, like it's fucking funny. My girlfriend is gone. I hope you rot in fucking hell!"

The teenagers confirmed that Paul was the one who had been driving the boat. The police officers looked at Paul and saw problems ahead. "You know Alex Murdaugh? That's his son. Good luck!"

The young boaters were taken to the hospital. They had spent the evening drinking. Paul was much more drunk than the others. The police wanted to know who had been at the helm of the boat, Paul or Connor? They were getting ready to interrogate the Murdaugh boy when his father and grandfather showed up at the hospital. Randolph Murdaugh III would be representing his grandson, starting now.

In the corridor, Alex Murdaugh spoke to the police officers, a prosecutor's badge hanging from his waistband. He tried to look in on each of the young people and knocked on the door of their hospital rooms. He counseled Connor, especially, to say nothing. He would take care of everything.

A week after the accident, Mallory Beach's body was recovered in a swamp, several miles from the bridge. The teens in the boat had all named Paul as the driver.

In his deposition, Connor Cook mentioned rumors concerning the Murdaugh family. According to one rumor, Paul had pushed the housekeeper down the front steps of the house. She'd died and there had never been an investigation. According to another rumor, Paul had somehow been implicated in a story about a guy found lying dead in the middle of the road, but Paul had gotten away with it.

In April 2019, Paul was charged with "involuntary homicide and driving a boat under the influence of alcohol." In a packed courtroom, he pleaded not guilty. The Murdaughs called on Dick Harpootlian, one of the most powerful lawyers in South Carolina, a rock star in his parish, and a Democratic senator known to play golf with Joe Biden. Paul was released from prison on a $50,000 bond. Four local journalists—Mandy Matney, John Mark, Michael DeWitt, and Will Folks—unraveled this emblematic story of the systemic injustice that was eating away at this corner of the United States like gangrene. They wondered, were the Murdaughs going to get away with this? The question remained unanswered. Paul's trial would never take place.

Just one day after the murders of Maggie and Paul, on June 8, 2021, police announced in a press release that the good citizens of Hampton County were in no danger. It was a polite way to communicate that this was a matter concerning the Murdaughs alone. Journalists, lawyers, and residents began trying to connect the dots. Of course the family had enemies, but who would have had a motivation for pulling the trigger? Had someone who wanted to harm them hired a killer? Or was this the work of an unhinged individual who was worked up after the events of the boat accident were covered in the press and on social media? Or was the murder an act of reprisal for the death of Stephen Smith, who was found dead on the road? Or for the death of the housekeeper?

While locals wrestled with these questions, the police made progress. On August 11, 2021, just two months after the murders, Alex Murdaugh once again found himself face-to-face with Detective David Owen.

Sitting in his office with gray carpeting, a brown table, and black chairs, the lawyer wore a bright blue polo shirt and gray trousers. His glasses were shoved up on his head, and he sat with his legs and arms crossed. Officer Owen had questions, as promised. "Of course," said Murdaugh. He rolled out his version of his day on June 7, 2021. He went to work. After returning home at the end of the day, he spent some time with Paul, and they talked about this and that. Then they joined Maggie for dinner. And after that? "I laid down on the couch and dozed off." When he woke up, he went to visit his mother, then went back to Moselle, as he'd already said. As he recounted the evening, tears came to his eyes.

Detective Owen went to find a box of tissues, and the lawyer patted him on the shoulder.

"Can you do this?"

"I can do it."

Now, the police wanted to show him a video posted on Snapchat a few hours before the murders. Paul had filmed his father while they were roaming around the estate. In the video, Alex was trying to straighten up a tree, which kept dropping again each time he let go. Paul could be heard laughing off camera. It wasn't clear exactly what they were doing, but that's not what interested the investigators. During these few seconds, they noted, Alex had been wearing a bright blue polo shirt and khaki pants. When the police arrived at the crime scene, however, he was dressed in a white T-shirt and khaki shorts. At what point had he changed his clothes? "I don't really remember," answered Alex. "Probably when I came back to the house."

What did the timeline say? At approximately 8:40 p.m., Paul was at the kennel and called his friend Rogan, who thought he could hear Alex's voice in the background. The question was, had Alex stopped at the kennel after dinner but before leaving to visit his mother?

"No, sir, not if my times are correct."

Nearly two hours later, as the interrogation was ending, Detective Owen asked his final questions, which were the most difficult to hear and ask.

"Did you kill Maggie?"

"Did I kill my wife?"

"Yes."

"No, David, I did not kill my wife."

"Do you know who did?"

"No, I don't know."

"Did you kill Paul?"

"No, I did not kill Paul."

"Do you know who did?"

"No, I don't know who did."

A short silence, then Alex Murdaugh returned the questions.

"Do you think I killed Maggie?"

Agent Owen raised his arms in a shrug. "I have to go where the facts lead me."

"Do you think I killed Paul?"

"I have to go where the evidence leads me. And I have nothing that points to somebody else at this time."

"Does that mean I'm a suspect?"

"I have to put my beliefs aside and go with the facts," repeated Officer Owen for a third time.

Murdaugh nodded.

Where did the facts lead? Three months after the murders and barely three weeks after this interrogation, Alex Murdaugh again dialed 911, at 1:30 p.m. on September 4, 2021. What he said was astonishing. The murderer was back. And this time, the murderer was after him.

3

THE SIDE OF THE ROAD

In the calm voice of a man now used to enduring hell, Alex Murdaugh told the operator how he had just had a close brush with death.

On Labor Day, while driving down Old Salkehatchie Road, a narrow route that runs through the woods and past properties where trees had been cleared, one of his tires blew not far from a little Baptist church. He was out inspecting the damage when suddenly a car stopped and some guy took a shot at him.

"Oh, okay," said the operator. "Were you shot?"

"Yes. But I'm okay."

"Did they actually shoot you, or did they try to shoot you?"

"They shot me. I'm bleeding a lot," he added.

"What part of your body?" asked the operator.

"I'm not sure. Somewhere on my head."

Once again, the police started their engines. A helicopter took off. An ambulance was dispatched. Stripped to the waist, lying on the stretcher in the back of the vehicle with a blood pressure cuff on his arm and a brace on his neck, Alex Murdaugh reported this rather peculiar story to the investigators. A car drove past, made a U-turn, and a "really nice" man stopped to help him, said Alex. Alex turned toward his car, and that's when the Good Samaritan turned into a butcher. The muffled shot sounded like a clap of thunder. "Extremely loud." A rifle, for sure.

The Hampton County police officers could discern no visible wound. Alex Murdaugh had only a superficial scrape, as if the bullet had grazed his skull on its way into the pine trees. He was lucky. The helicopter took off, transporting him to the emergency room.

At the hospital, Alex told the same story again. First his car had hit some kind of debris on the roadway and his tire blew, so he stopped. A dark-colored pickup truck drove past, made a U-turn, and the driver got out to ask if he needed a hand, which was nice. Then, pow! After that, Alex Murdaugh lost his vision. But not his memory. If he saw the man who had wanted his hide, he would recognize him, he was sure of it. His assailant was white, around thirty or forty, clean-shaven with short hair. The officers made a police sketch and started a search for him.

They combed through the high grass along the road. There was no sign of debris that would result in a flat tire. However, on the other side of the road, they found a small gray pocketknife. They also obtained the surveillance footage from the security cameras mounted on the little Baptist church just up the road—a valuable piece of evidence. Studying the images from that day would allow them to isolate Alex Murdaugh's vehicle, as well as that of his mysterious attacker. *Let's take a look.*

At about 1:25 p.m., a dark-colored pickup truck drives through the frame, followed by Alex Murdaugh's automobile twenty seconds later. Five minutes after that, the pickup truck drives back through, headed in the other direction. He has turned around to come back. The truck has a gold fender, easy to recognize. Odd.

Even more odd was that two days after the incident, on the evening of September 6, Agent Owen received a telephone call from Randy Murdaugh. He just wanted to let the police know that his younger brother Alex was behaving strangely. Could he be more specific? Alex kept trying to talk the nurses and the medical personnel into lending him a telephone—even offering them money in return. He had managed to make several phone calls. One of the numbers led to Curtis Edward Smith, a distant cousin.

On the morning of September 7, police drove to the residence of one Curtis "Eddie" Smith, who lived in a modest house with a front porch. A pickup truck with a gold fender was parked out front, exactly like the one seen in the video surveillance footage. The police officers knocked at the door. The man who answered was sixty-one years old, with a white mop of hair tending toward blond, a gray beard, a half-restless, half-short-tempered gaze, and a glower that didn't immediately come across as friendly. To his friends, he was "Fast Eddie."

The police search of his house that followed turned up drugs. Also, a pharmaceuticals manual, receipts, and a spiral notebook filled with notes that looked like a sales ledger. Curtis "Eddie" Smith had a feeling he would need to talk to his lawyer—who was no other than Alex Murdaugh.

After this dramatic turn of events, there was another unexpected development. Through his two lawyers, Alex

Murdaugh announced that he was admitting himself to a residential drug treatment center. The sad truth, which he had concealed for too long, was that this prominent Moselle citizen had suffered from an addiction to oxycodone for over two decades—oxycodone, a powerful opioid painkiller. He could no longer control his addiction and regretted many things in his life.

He claimed that he was now prepared to clear up this cursed incident at the side of the road. From the treatment center in Atlanta, he responded to investigators by speakerphone, flanked by his two lawyers. He was sorry to have given them the runaround—he wasn't himself. And anyway, he was going to explain everything.

The story began on September 3, on the eve of his supposed attack at the side of the road. That day, Alex Murdaugh had been forced to resign from his position at his law firm, after a meeting in which his associates accused him of embezzling serious money—several million dollars. For someone who had lost his wife and son only a few months before, the news was too much. "I told myself that it would be better if I weren't here anymore," confided Murdaugh to the investigators. He concocted an almost perfect plan.

He'd make his suicide look like a murder so Buster, his older son and only remaining immediate relative, would receive the $10 million from his life insurance policy. But who could he count on in a situation like this? That's why he called his cousin Eddie on the morning of September 4. To ask him a little favor.

Curtis Edward Smith and Alex Murdaugh were two men on opposite trajectories. The son of a marine, Eddie had been born in the swamps of Beaufort, fifty miles southwest of Hampton, then was hauled back and forth between North Carolina and Mississippi. After high school, he held a string of working-class jobs that left him with a bad back. Like so many other Americans at the turn of the twenty-first century, he turned to oxycodone to keep his pain under control.

That worked so well that he started selling to others as a dealer. His customers soon included his distant cousin Alex Murdaugh. Sometimes the lawyer paid him in cash, sometimes by check—ometimes for forty, fifty, sixty thousand dollars in pills at a time, Murdaugh confessed to the police. Then came the morning of September 4, at which point the two men's stories diverged.

This was the version that Murdaugh gave from the treatment center. First, he set up a meeting place with Eddie in Almeda, not far from his mother's house. They met at a service station. Alex told his cousin Eddie that he was in a very bad way and asked his dealer-cousin to shoot him. "At first, he was a little surprised, then he said okay," Alex said. They drove down the road in tandem, then parked in the same place as before. Curtis "Eddie" Smith handed Alex his knife, and Alex planted it in the back tire of his car. Then he handed his accomplice his .38-caliber handgun and turned around, waiting for the shot and death . . . and that was it.

Officer Ryan Kelly took notes and then asked a few more questions.

"You say that you paid him for the pills, but you didn't pay him to shoot you?"

"Correct."

"I'm going to be honest, that doesn't make any sense."

"I understand."

The police officer continued trying to summarize what he had just heard.

"So, you made an agreement that he would shoot you. That way, your suicide would look like a murder with aggravated theft and all that, just so your son would receive the life insurance money."

"I'm not sure about the theft, but the rest is right."

His cousin Eddie's version wasn't complicated by the interrogation room secret concerning the allegations of embezzlement. Eddie was the dealer and alleged hitman, a larger-than-life redneck. This character was too perfect for ABC, NBC, and CBS to let him get away. So, with a new business-suited lawyer at his side, Eddie stood in front of their cameras and delivered his truth on the man he'd loved "like a brother" until then.

On the morning of September 4, he began, Alex Murdaugh had set up a meeting with him but was vague on its purpose. The two men met.

"You're going to shoot me," said Alex.

"No," said Eddie.

Alex, who had a revolver in his hand, made a move to turn the gun on himself. Eddie grabbed his hand, and they struggled for control of the .38. That's when a shot went off and Alex dropped to the ground. At that point, Eddie grabbed the revolver, checked to be sure everything was okay, and left. "So he wasn't shot in the head?" asked a reporter.

"No, if I'd shot him, he would be dead."

Americans adored Curtis "Eddie" Smith and wanted more. In the following weeks, journalists from the *New York Post* and the *New Yorker* went to his house to interview Curtis "Eddie" Smith with his cats named Biggie and Jay-Z and his pit bull named Dixie. The pill dealer offered his best side to the photographers, proud to pose for them on his front stoop. "It was the craziest situation I'd ever been involved in," he said, summing up the situation to the Yanks who were passing through.

Alas, the party didn't last long. On September 16, 2021, the two men appeared at a hearing at the Hampton County police station. They were dressed in gray-beige prison jumpsuits, their hands were cuffed and they wore masks as a precaution against COVID. Alex Murdaugh stood accused of orchestrating his own suicide. "He had fallen into disgrace," said his lawyer, Dick Harpootlian. "If you're wondering what opioid addiction looks like, you have it, here, right before your eyes." Curtis "Eddie" Smith stood accused of assisted suicide, insurance fraud, dealing methamphetamines, and possession of marijuana. The investigators had followed the money and tracked the connections linking the cousins with little difficulty.

According to the indictment, between 2013 and 2021, Curtis "Eddie" Smith had accepted 437 checks signed by Alex Murdaugh. The amounts had increased exponentially over the eight years, for a total of $2.5 million. From May 7 to June 7, 2021—that is, during the month that preceded the murders of Maggie and Paul—Alex Murdaugh had allegedly sent his cousin $130,000. In the days leading up to the strange incident at the side of the road, Alex had sent his cousin $25,600.

Questions led to other questions: Where was all this money coming from? And where had it gone?

On October 14, 2021, Alex Murdaugh was arrested as he exited the detox center and was charged with embezzlement of the money belonging to Gloria Satterfield's children. The police opened an investigation into the housekeeper's death and were preparing to exhume her body.

Alex Murdaugh was incarcerated at the Richland County jail. In the months to come, a cascade of about one hundred charges would be brought against him. Thirty-some counts of embezzlement, dozens of computer crimes, money laundering, tax evasion, and falsification of documents. In all, the lawyer stood accused of embezzling $9 million. That July 14, he was indicted for the murders of Maggie and Paul.

In the space of two years, this ordinary, respected local public figure had become the supervillain of a saga that had America mesmerized. Tabloid journalists descended on Hampton County. Amateur investigators joined the game. Social media latched onto the case. Theories proliferated on the "Murdaugh Uncensored" Reddit thread. "What if the side of the road was actually the end of the road?" someone asked on YouTube. On the internet, Alex Murdaugh had become an evil character and a meme.

Mark Seal, a prominent figure in new journalism and author of *Leave the Gun, Take the Cannoli: The Epic Story of the Making of* The Godfather, attacked the Murdaughs. Investigative journalist Mandy Matney launched the *Murdaugh Murders Podcast*, which became one of the most listened-to programs in the United States (she later sold the rights to Hulu). Netflix also launched a three-part documentary, signing exclusive contracts with the witnesses they questioned.

For HBO, it was just buy-in-the-room, a term used by producers to designate projects launched on the basis of a pitch. Producer Brooke Brunson was assigned to the project. She mastered the Lowcountry like she'd mastered Hollywood. She was best known for her work on the first three films of the *Pirates of the Caribbean.* When explaining why she had accepted this project, she responded without hesitation. "This story is stranger than fiction."

PART 2
MURDAUGHPALOOZA

4

TRUE CRIME, USA

A lonely nail protruded from the wall. At the back of a courtroom upstairs in the Colleton County Courthouse, a painting had been removed from its hook even though it had hung there for decades. The oil painting in question portrayed a wise old man seated at an angle, dressed in a black suit with a red necktie. This was Randolph Murdaugh, grandfather of Alex and commonly known as Buster.

Seated in the rows of benches and facing the empty space on the wall sat three people in prayer. They were praying for the weeks to come, praying for protection from evil, and praying for light at that time of confusion. They were praying for the strength to get through the approaching storm. Afterward, one of them, a small woman with a pearl necklace and palm tree earrings, opened her serene brown eyes. She was Rebecca "Becky" Hill, the court clerk.

"So, it's really going to be chaos?" an employee asked her.

"Yes. It's going to be chaos."

In the early days of 2023, a strange kind of hurricane was about to hit the region: the murder trial of Alex Murdaugh. This attorney would be judged in the small, pleasant town of Walterboro, with its five thousand residents, antique shops, rice festival, and charming streets that had been used as sets for films and feel-good movies like *Forrest Gump*. A few days before the storm made landfall, residents braced themselves for the weeks ahead. It was hard to make out the palm trees in the gloom, and the Spanish moss hung from the oaks in long, sad beards.

In a vacant lot, municipal employees were unloading barriers from a pickup truck and began setting them up. Residents had advertised their houses or campers on Airbnb, renting them for over one hundred dollars a night. There were no vacancies at the motels. Restaurants had changed their hours to correspond to the trial. "This will bring in customers, for sure," predicted one merchant. "Nobody knows what to expect," said a woman with red-dyed hair who had just opened a shop selling pottery and car parts. Hard to determine the thought process that had led her to set up a big wooden sign on the sidewalk where passersby could stick their heads through the hole to pose for a souvenir photo as a cowboy astride a giant chicken with the message "I was at the Alex Murdaugh trial." A keepsake for later, when all this would be just a memory.

On the highway, one billboard recommended a local lawyer to contact in the case of a car accident. Another one advised REPENT! in huge letters. Everyone in town dreaded the impending arrival of what they called "the circus."

The official guide, Scott Grooms, was wearing cargo pants and power washing the historic building that was to house the teams from Channel 4. With a full head of neatly combed white hair, the director of the Walterboro tourist office looked like a man with a sunny disposition. He loved this town. He'd grown up here. When he moved somewhere else, he didn't like it and moved back. "The day we moved back, neighbors helped us unload the moving van," he said. He liked journalists too. For thirty-five years, he'd had a career as a weatherman on television, where he'd covered tornadoes and huge golf tournaments. He'd started preparing for the trial six months before.

Across from the courthouse, Scott had transformed the all-purpose room of the Wildlife Center, a building housing reptiles and amphibians of the region, into a media space. Coffee would flow nonstop into Styrofoam cups, the refrigerator would be filled with Diet Pepsi, and the Wi-Fi would be top-notch. In December, Scott Grooms had posted a call on Facebook to food trucks in the region. That was a stroke of genius.

For the residents who found his announcement inappropriate, he related his experience while working on the Susan Smith trial in 1995. That was the mother convicted of drowning her two children and who had tried to pin it on a Black man, claiming he'd kidnapped them during a carjacking. "It was in a small town with no place to eat except a fast food restaurant and a grocery store." Fox News would be sending a team of forty people. "It adds up fast," he said. Close to a thousand reporters, producers, technicians, authors, and true crime fans were expected. The air was electric, and the noise from the pressure washer tore through the quiet.

A year and a half after the murders of Maggie and Paul, the whole country lay in suspense, awaiting the outcome of a tortuous saga that had been difficult to wrap their minds around. The plot could be summarized in this way: it was the story *of* an America in decline *in* an America in decline. In the hearing room at the courthouse, technicians set up three camera angles and the latest microphones. The trial would be streamed on Court TV in real time, with a slight delay for commercial breaks.

On the second floor, Becky Hill was ironing out the final details. The court clerk would be the mistress of ceremonies for the weeks to come. All decisions—both large and small—had to go through her. Would journalists be allowed to set up their tents on the lawn? That was a no. Would cellphones be allowed inside the courthouse? Also no. Should they order some ginger ale to have it on hand? Of course. "Thank you, Miss Becky," said the employees as they came out of her office. The turquoise walls and the mantras about positive thinking gave a glimpse into the collective state of mind driving Walterboro. The world was watching, so it was the time to show the best of themselves.

On January 23, the circus began at five o'clock in the morning. Shadowy figures got to work outside the courthouse. Though it was still dark outside, technicians pulled carts piled high with crates and unspooled cables and set up tripods, tents, and camp chairs. Generators rumbled on the sidewalk. Tall satellite antennae overlooked a lineup of vehicles parked in the big vacant lot—vans with WSAV, ABC, and LIVE 5 NEWS, and

SUVs with license plates from as far away as Texas and Nebraska.

At 6:30 a.m., an anchorwoman fixed her hair while reading her notes on an iPhone. A school bus rumbled past in the street. A young man took a selfie with his index finger raised.

Around nine o'clock, a procession of black cars drove into the parking lot behind the courthouse. Photographers gathered. One man was holding a cross high with JESUS SAVES written across it. Reporters tapped away on their iPhones. The back door of a van opened, and Alex Murdaugh stepped out from a little cage. He was wearing a white dress shirt over a T-shirt. His legs were swimming in gray trousers, and he wore a suit jacket with gold buttons that covered the handcuffs on his wrists.

Becky Hill glanced out her office window. Things were looking more organized than she would have imagined. Her cell phone rang with the first few notes of "Come and Get Your Love."

In the courtroom, the seats reserved for the top guns were labeled on the back of a row of benches—some journalists would later refer to it as the "bunker."

Will Folks was there, the creator of the investigation site FITSNews. His smooth skull made him look both cool and serious, as if he had always had a source in advance. Valerie Bauerlein, a well-known journalist from the *Wall Street Journal*, had come to write her own version of *In Cold Blood*. Nancy Grace, the famous Nancy Grace, host of *Crime Stories with Nancy Grace*, and whose IMDb page indicated that she had played herself in *Batman v Superman*, would also be making the trip.

Regional figures were also there, one of whom was Michael DeWitt of the *Hampton County Guardian* in his signature plaid shirt. At the time, he was writing two books in addition to all the articles on the trial that he would write in his silver-gray Ford pickup truck since the newspaper had sold off its newsroom to save money. Older and still more legendary was John Monk of the daily newspaper *The State*, who had dedicated a good part of his career to making South Carolina face its racist past. His white hair was askew, and eight pens stuck out of his breast pocket. He referred to the special correspondents coming from all corners of the country and elsewhere as "the parachutes."

Behind these stars were all strata of journalists: local TV anchors, national producers, investigation experts, and the tabloids. A young man with a kid's face in an adult suit asked for information on how to obtain a press pass. His name was James, and he was the creator of a YouTube channel called James From Court. After following the Johnny Depp and Amber Heard trial, he was planning to comment on the Alex Murdaugh trial on Twitch for $200 per live stream. In the media space at the Wildlife Center, someone asked for the Wi-Fi password, and someone else told him it was "walterbororocks."

For South Carolina, it was the trial of the century. The lawyers had pulled out their best pin-striped suits. Eric Bland, the lawyer representing Gloria Satterfield's children, took selfies with fans of his podcast *Cup of Justice*. Justin Bamberg, the lawyer representing a number of the victims of Alex Murdaugh's presumed embezzlement, never went anywhere without his gold watch and alligator skin loafers. He had made a weapon of his name, with his slogan, "Need a lawyer who will fight for you? Bam!"

Connor Cook's lawyer, Joe McCulloch, with his white mane and soft blue eyes, gave as many interviews as possible, like an actor promoting a film. He had slipped a copy of *Rolling Stone* magazine into his bag—with superstar Rosalía on the cover, he asked if she was any good—in case he got bored, which seemed unlikely. In addition to his work, McCulloch was writing a screenplay based on the case, which he hoped to sell to Hollywood. To outsiders just passing through, he'd say, "South Carolina is too small for a republic but too large for an insane asylum." The quote had been uttered by illustrious prosecutor James L. Petigru in the early days of the Civil War. For McCulloch, it summed up the events leading to this day and what was likely to happen in the weeks to come.

Leading the prosecution was Creighton Waters, a lawyer standing 5'7" with a short nose, a gray goatee, and a look of fury. Before diving into this case heart and soul, he had been the guitarist for a rock band called Sole Purpose, which played covers for birthdays and weddings. He had a little rhetorical trick up his sleeve, which he planned to test at the stand—asking witnesses if they knew Alex Murdaugh and then asking them if they *really* knew Alex Murdaugh. He was convinced it would have some effect.

Prosecutor Alan Wilson would also be present. He was a Republican, a Trumper, and had his eye on getting himself elected governor. He knew a victory by the State in this trial of the century would be a feather in his cap.

On the defense side stood the Democrat Dick Harpootlian, known as "Poot," who had been close to the client and his family since the beginning of the case.

Americans had learned his name in 1983 when he'd sent Donald "Pee Wee" Gaskins, South Carolina's most famous serial killer in history, to the electric chair. Since then, Harpootlian had argued about a hundred murder cases, which made him a point of reference on the subject. Why this appetite for crime? "Listen, I like it," he retorted, cutting off further discussion. "It's why I get up in the morning."

The lawyers all knew one another, used first names, and slapped one another on the back. Harpootlian and McCulloch were old friends. Harpootlian appreciated McCulloch's humor and joked back by rubbing his eye with his middle finger to give McCulloch the salute. On this day, Dick Harpootlian was celebrating his seventy-fourth birthday. McCulloch planned to mark the occasion with a tin of caviar.

"What do you call those little round pancakes?"

Blinis.

"All rise!" ordered the security guard. All those present stood, and Judge Clifton Newman, a man radiating casual sophistication and a charisma polished by the years, took his seat in the large leather armchair. Born into a family of farmers, he was the nephew of civil rights activist Isaiah DeQuincey Newman. He had attended segregated schools before climbing step-by-step to the magistrature and inspiring a whole generation of African American lawyers. He seemed the very antithesis of Murdaugh, presiding over the duel between the State of South Carolina and defendant Richard Alexander Murdaugh.

But the public would have to wait patiently a little longer. Before the trial itself could begin, jury selection had to take place. Over the next two days, nine hundred people were called to resolve the giant problem of finding twelve just and impartial individuals to serve. One by one, Clifton Newman and Becky Hill asked them to stand and state their juror number, their marital status, and their profession. There were construction workers, an Amazon delivery man, a truck driver, a post office employee, a supermarket employee, a high school teacher, a retiree, a veteran . . .

A few looked disheveled, their faces tired. Some of them had gotten up at dawn to take care of their children or ailing family members; others suffered from post-traumatic stress, anxiety, or back problems that prevented them from sitting or standing for too long.

Jurors were paid twenty dollars a day. Some of them did everything possible to get out of there as soon as possible. "I'm the one who signs employee paychecks," said one. "If I'm not there, I'm liable to get shot." The catch was that the less they wanted to be there, the better, more impartial jurors they were likely to be.

"If you have already heard about this case," said the judge, "please stand." The benches at the back of the room creaked as everyone stood up. They were asked to list their news sources. Juror 45: the local news. Juror 148: Facebook. Juror 149: podcasts and YouTube. Juror 220: the internet and the radio. Juror 821: television and social media. Juror 879: articles that come up on the screen. Juror 886: conversations at the café.

"Everything they already said," one woman summed up.

Second question: "Who knows the Murdaughs?" The benches creaked again. "He sued my father," said one man. Another detailed his family tree. One young man said he knew Paul Murdaugh well.

"Do you think that could affect your judgment?"

"Yes, it could."

One more down. The judge then read a list of the 250 people who might be brought in to testify during the trial: around a hundred people from law enforcement, from county police to the FBI, members of the Murdaugh family, friends of Alex Murdaugh, his associates, and his clients. It took ten minutes to read the list. If the jury candidates knew any of these people, they had to indicate it, and the room emptied out a little more. If they'd needed to highlight the importance of the Murdaugh family in the region one last time, this scene illustrated it perfectly.

Finally, Judge Clifton Newman asked the accused to rise and face those assembled. Alex Murdaugh stood up and turned his face, the face of a man without qualities, toward the courtroom. His pink complexion leaned toward gray, his forehead was creased, and his eyes were small dark marbles onto which everyone could project their own opinion.

“Good afternoon,” he said.

“Good afternoon,” came a few scattered responses.

A slight sense of ill ease ran through the courtroom. However, it really did seem like a kickoff.

5

NOT EVERYBODY CRIES

The poor-quality images projected on several screens might contain a grain of truth, or they might not. But this was what had Americans holding their collective breath on January 25, 2023. For the first day of the actual trial, the judge had decided to project the video footage from the evening of June 7, 2021, in the Walterboro courtroom exactly as it had been filmed at the scene by the police body cams. When the camera fell on the victims, the lawyers covered the monitors with sheets of paper to prevent those assembled from seeing the mutilated bodies.

As the nightmare came back to him again, Alex fluctuated between two moods. Expression 1: hunched on his chair, crying and rocking his head forward and back, an expression of horror on his red face. Expression 2: paging through documents, whispering to his team, and following the trial over his frameless glasses like the lawyer he'd once been. During the breaks, he smiled easily.

Sitting on the benches behind him were his sister, Lynn; his little brother, John Marvin; his older brother, Randy; and his older son, Buster, a young man with wavy red hair and an impassive face. At the beginning of the trial, father and son greeted each other with a slight nod.

The police officers came to the stand. Since Colleton County is a small region, some of them were also performing security duty at the trial. Sergeant Daniel Greene, the first to arrive at the crime scene, described what he had seen—tears and blood on the clothes.

"He seemed upset," he said, referring to the accused, "but I wouldn't say panicky."

Corporal Chad McDowell confirmed this. Alex Murdaugh really had asked him, "How ya doin'?" Deputy Jason Chapman saw no tears either. "Not everybody cries. I have no problem with that," he said.

It was now time for Dick Harpootlian to move his first pawns on the board. The defense lawyer put the video on pause and asked the officers to explain how they proceeded to secure a crime scene like this. To

Corporal McDowell, Dick Harpootlian snapped, "You don't know what you are doing there. Specifically, if your work consisted in securing the scene, why do we see officers coming and going across the screen without bags over their shoes?"

"We did our best not to contaminate the area," said Sergeant Greene. Yet the print of a police officer's shoe was found in the blood.

"You call that doing your best? Walking around in the place where there's blood and brain?" continued the lawyer in a calm voice, sorry for them. To no one in particular, he asked exactly what kind of training they had received to botch the job like this.

"It's very basic, what you would get at the criminal justice academy," answered McDowell.

"Very basic," repeated Harpootlian.

You could call that winning the first round.

Analysis of the clothing also raised questions for the lawyer. When police officers arrived, Alex Murdaugh was wearing, it had already been established, a white T-shirt and khaki shorts. Those clothes had been seized. First, an expert noted that the T-shirt showed blood spatters. But then another expert thought it would be difficult to identify the "high-speed spatters" that were to be expected when someone was shot at point-blank range.

Detective Laura Rutland came to the stand. She had been present at the first interrogation, the one conducted at 1:00 a.m. At that time, Alex Murdaugh was sweaty, she said, but his clothes were dry, like when someone has just taken a quick shower in full summer. Then it came back to her that the accused had changed his clothes in the course of the evening. Murdaugh had told the police officers that he'd taken both victims' pulse, touched their bodies, and even tried to move them. John Meadors, the prosecuting attorney and a combination of Lieutenant Columbo and the actor Mark Ruffalo, scratched his head as if trying to understand. He got down on his knees and patted the floor, mimicking a man taking the pulse of his wife who lay in a pool of blood.

"How would you describe the defendant's hands?" he finally asked the detective.

"They were clean."

"How would you describe his arms?"

"They were clean."

"How would you describe his T-shirt?"

"Clean."

"How would you describe his shorts?"

"Clean."

"How would you describe his shoes?"

"They were clean."

The score was tied, 1–1.

On to the rifles. The prosecutor opened a stack of boxes and brought out weapons one after another, all of them seized at the Murdaugh residence: a pump rifle, a .12-gauge shotgun, a semiautomatic rifle with thermal scope to hunt nocturnal game, and others.

"Objection, Your Honor!" The defense contested this parade of long guns, like so many snakes. The objection was overruled since the prosecution needed to demonstrate the breadth of its research into the means by which the murders had been committed.

After comparing six casings found near Maggie's body to casings found elsewhere on the property, the investigators were prepared to establish that Alex's wife had been killed by a rifle belonging to the family, a 300 Blackout AR-15 assault rifle, which had disappeared. As for the .12-gauge shotgun that had killed Paul, the Murdaughs owned three Benelli Super Black Eagles. One of them belonged to Paul—the weapon that Alex had right near him when the police arrived. The second one had been seized by the police the day after the murders, and the third was Alex's favorite rifle, which had also vanished into thin air.

The defense lawyer took the floor. Why would Alex Murdaugh have used two different weapons to kill his wife and son, just a few seconds apart?

Dick Harpootlian presented a large panel that showed the victims in silhouette to drive home his point about the trajectory of the bullets and the angle at which the victims had been shot.

"One possible explanation would be that there were two shooters, correct?" he asked a stunned officer of the South Carolina Law Enforcement Division (SLED). She nodded and answered yes in a barely audible voice. His tone implying that this was obvious, Harpootlian repeated, "One possible explanation would be two shooters." She shrugged as though she didn't know and started to respond, but he cut her off. "Not the only explanation, but a reasonable explanation, like that of a single shooter, correct?"

"Yes."

Hands in his pockets and face frozen in a frown of disapproval, Dick Harpootlian had a way of looking chronically grumpy but also completely relaxed. Probing one gray area after another, he realized that his work in this trial could be summed up as sowing seeds of doubt. Then anything might happen. For his client to avoid conviction, all they needed was for a single juror to waver. And for that to happen, Alex Murdaugh would also have to avoid traps.

6

A CHICKEN IN THE CHOPS

Three days after the murders, Alex Murdaugh was questioned in Officer David Owen's car for the second time. He cleared his throat repeatedly. For the first few minutes, the atmosphere was fairly relaxed.

"Where are you coming from?" he asked Officer Jeff Croft, who was sitting behind him.

"Barnwell."

"Really? I have some cousins who live in Barnwell."

The interrogation began, and again, Alex told the whole story from the beginning, keeping to his initial version. On Monday, June 7, 2021, he hung around the house all morning. Then he went to work. At the end of the day, he and Paul took their tour around the property. Maggie came home. All three had dinner together.

Then Maggie and Paul went down to the kennel. He lay down on the couch and dozed off before going to visit his mother. A few minutes into the interview, he opened the car door to spit. "Where were we?" he asked. "I left to go over to my mother's house. I came home. I went inside. Nobody was there. I got back in the car. I went down to the kennel. And then . . . you know . . ."

From the back seat, Officer Croft asked, summarizing, "The last time you saw Paul and Maggie was at dinner?"

"Yes, sir."

In the Colleton County Courthouse on January 30, 2023, the video of this second interrogation was being projected during the trial. At the back of the courtroom, behind the witnesses and the high-profile attendees, the public struggled to follow. The assembly was composed mostly of white women over thirty-five years old, which, for many sociological reasons detailed in various studies, corresponds to the traditional consumer of true crime documentaries, podcasts, and books.

Alison, wearing a black and gray vest, had made the trip from Tennessee to see the characters from her favorite series. She asked the people around her if they had seen any stars. As for herself, she'd had her photo taken with lawyer Eric Bland, which she'd sent to her daughter to make her jealous.

Mark, a guy with a fringe of long, black hair that ringed his bald pate, lived in Los Angeles and wrote screenplays. He'd been in the area and decided to make a detour to spend some time there. He said that it would be good for his imagination. For the same reason, he sometimes attended Trump rallies.

Bob and Rose, a retired couple from Florida, had booked a motel room in Walterboro to spend a few days attending the trial of the century.

Marze had come down from Alexandria, Virginia, which was a seven-hour drive. She was getting ready to move to South Carolina. While waiting for her house to be built, she planned to attend the trial as much as possible.

They all made the same observation. They couldn't see or hear as well in the courtroom as they could on television. "Can you hear what's happening?" whispered Jerry to his wife. A few minutes passed. "Are you still interested?"

Alex Murdaugh's voice blended with the hum of the air-conditioning, the crinkle of candy wrappers, and the rattle of Tic Tacs that helped the public stay awake. Occasionally, someone nodded off. During a break, one man pressed his hands to his thighs, swiveled back and forth on his hips, and advised his neighbors to do the same. The goal was to stay alert as they waited for what journalists, lawyers, and crime junkies called "bombs."

Suddenly, one of them hit. Forty-five minutes into the video of that interrogation, Alex Murdaugh broke down, looking at a photo of Paul's body. Alex said it was terrible. It sounded like he was saying, "It's so bad, I did him so bad."

What? Mark frowned and turned to Alison. Journalists exchanged glances and read the same doubt in their neighbors' eyes. The excerpt was played again, and they strained to hear better.

"It's so bad, *I* did him so bad." Or else, "It's so bad, *they* did him so bad." "I hurt him?" "They hurt him?" No one was certain, but everyone was alert. Had the accused confessed to murdering his son?

Nancy Grace's team was ready. Given the humidity, a makeup artist had to empty a can of hairspray to hold the celebrity's hair in place. She was typing on her phone in its pink case, ignoring the color being dabbed on her eyelids. The new episode of her podcast would be titled "Murdaugh Bombshell: 'I did him so bad.'"

The next day, the excerpt was replayed again and again. Special Agent Jeff Croft, who had been sitting in the back seat of the squad car during the interrogation, was categorical. He'd heard "I." "I did him so bad." Jim Griffin, the defense lawyer, asked him if he was sure. Affirmative.

What happened after that? What had he done? "I made a mental note," answered the special agent. That's all. Why hadn't he followed up for specifics? And if it was a confession, why hadn't he handcuffed Murdaugh?

At this point, the defense replayed the excerpt, slowing it down to one-third the real speed, which increased the confusion. Objectively, it was difficult to make it out. So, let's say that he did say "I." Exactly what did he mean by that? That he had killed Paul? That he had hurt his son? Or just that he had failed as a father?

Alex Murdaugh sat motionless on his bench, but on his lips, people could read him saying, "I did not say that." Everyone held their breath, and yet no one knew that the most important part of the June 10, 2021, interrogation was still to come.

There were the cell phones. Information technology and cell phone data experts took the stand and detailed the final communications, the number of steps recorded, changes in screen orientation, and time stamps, which were precise down to the second. It was technical and essential to establishing the chronology of events.

First, Alex Murdaugh's cell phone. The phone registered no movement from 8:10 p.m. to 9:02 p.m. Then, at about the time when the defendant said he had left to visit his mother, Alex had called Maggie three times with no answer. Later that evening, at 9:45 p.m. and 10:04 p.m., he called her again. Still no answer. At 9:47 p.m., he texted her. "Call me, Honey."

According to the prosecution, none of these attempts had had any chance of reaching her: Maggie's and Paul's deaths had been estimated at around 8:50 p.m. Which led the investigators to Maggie's cell phone. At 8:49 p.m., it was locked. However, five minutes later, its screen orientation changed, switching from portrait to landscape. For the space of one second, the camera was activated, but the facial recognition mechanism did not unlock the telephone.

According to a technology expert, that seemed to indicate one thing: at that moment, someone other than Maggie was holding her phone. At 9:06:12 p.m., the screen again changed orientation, this time going back to portrait, as if someone was again holding the phone. Exactly two seconds later, Maggie received a call from

Alex. Had the defendant been holding his phone in one hand and his wife's phone in the other when she was already dead? Had he called to manufacture an alibi? The defense said no. The number of steps registered on the two phones did not correspond to this hypothesis.

After that, they turned to Paul's phone. It took investigators nine months to unlock it. In March 2022, a Secret Service agent used specialized software. Finding a four-digit code can require ten thousand attempts over a period of sixty-eight days, but the police ended up finding it after only three days. The password was a variation of Paul's birthday. What the investigators found in the phone surpassed all expectations.

On June 7, 2021, at 8:29 p.m., just twenty minutes before the presumed time of the murders, Paul received a text from his friend Megan saying, "You haven't sent me any recommendations for a movie." His response: "Ha ha, I didn't have a good one."

Ten minutes later, at 8:40 p.m., he received a call from his friend Rogan Gibson, who had asked the Murdaughs to take care of his Labrador, Cash. There seemed to be a problem with the dog's tail, which Paul and Rogan discussed for four minutes. At 8:44 p.m., Paul was at the kennel filming Cash so he could send the video to his friend. At 8:48 p.m., Paul recommended *A Star Is Born* to

Megan. Two more messages followed. "No, I need something happy," and "I don't like sad films." One minute later, the telephone was locked with only 2% battery power remaining, but Paul never read those messages.

A new bomb was about to drop—a video on Paul's phone. Fifty seconds were filmed at the kennel, between 8:44:49 and 8:45:47—in other words, just a few minutes before the estimated time of the murders. The prosecution was now going to show it to all in attendance. The benches creaked. Murmurs rippled through the courtroom as people leaned forward with anticipation.

The prosecutor pressed Play. On the screen, a hand could be seen opening a wire mesh door. A chocolate Labrador appeared, wagging his tail before the camera.

"Down. Down," said a first voice. It was Paul.

A second voice could be heard in the background. It was Maggie. "Hey, he has a bird in his mouth," she said, referring to a different dog, Bubba.

Then came the third voice, recognizable with its familiar Southern twang. "Come here, Bubba! Come here, Bubba!"

It was Alex Murdaugh. The video ended.

While the images played, Alex Murdaugh's head rocked forward and back. During the three interrogations, he'd kept repeating that he had not gone to the kennel with Maggie and Paul and the last time he'd seen them was at dinner. Here was a video that seemed to prove the opposite.

Rogan Gibson, Paul's friend and the owner of Cash, the chocolate Labrador, came to the stand. Gibson described his relationship to the Murdaughs, saying they were his second family. He had known them since he was eleven or twelve. He had a nickname for each member of the clan. "Bus" for Buster, "Big Red" for Alex, and "Miss Maggie" for Maggie. In November 2022, the police summoned Gibson to show him the video at the kennel. He recognized the voices of Paul, Maggie, and Alex, his second family.

On this eighth day of the trial, he was asked, on the stand, to confirm this under oath. He sat, head held high, jaw clenched. Alex Murdaugh stared hard at him over his glasses. Prosecutor Creighton Waters played the video again.

"Do you recognize your dog?"

"I recognize him."

"Do you recognize Paul's voice?"

"Yes, sir."

"Do you recognize Maggie's voice?"

"Yes, sir."

"Do you recognize Alex's voice?"

"Yes, sir."

"A hundred percent?"

"Yes, sir."

Only a week into the trial and already Alex Murdaugh had been caught red-handed lying on one of the most important details of the case. At 8:44 p.m., all three of them were at the kennel. A few minutes later, Maggie and Paul were dead, and Alex was alive. The logical conclusion did not play in his favor.

Gibson's response set off another round of questions, this time focusing on motive. Even if we suppose that Alex had committed the crimes, which seemed to be the case, why would the attorney have killed his wife and son? Pursuing this question was going to mean another trial that would require retracing the defendant's life, going into the details of his long list of financial crimes, and calling numerous new witnesses to the stand. God only knew when it would end.

In a meeting room, Becky Hill asked a clerk to order more sodas and more mini bottles of water. James From Court tried to figure out how to extend his stay in town. The circus had morphed into a vast swamp. Vehicle tires sank the electrical cables into the damp soil. "Fasten your seat belts," said Will Folks, the famous investigative journalist, as he strode past.

Nobody said it openly, but everyone seemed to be whispering it. To understand what was going on in Alex Murdaugh's mind on June 7, 2021, they were going to have to dig deep into his past and look toward the empty space on the courtroom wall where, not so long ago, the alleged murderer's ancestor had looked out over the crowd with an air of satisfaction.

PART 3
MURDAUGH COUNTRY

7

A CERTAIN CHARM

Sixty thousand men cleaved the countryside. On November 15, 1864, Union General William Tecumseh Sherman launched a savage, bloody, mounted military campaign. In addition to crushing the Confederate troops, he was determined to grind down the morale of the people of the South, leaving them with trauma that would last for generations. After passing through Atlanta, Sherman's troops swept toward the port of Savannah before veering north through South Carolina, forever haunting the land that had unleashed the War of Secession.

After Sherman passed, grass would no longer grow. His troops sowed terror and desolation, setting fire to farms, mills, sawmills, cotton gins, and rice plantations.

They stole horses, mules, livestock, supplied themselves from the harvests, pillaged houses. The enslaved were freed and masters were broken in the wake of pounding hooves, flames, and rifle shots. Civilians buried their most precious belongings at the bottom of swamps to save what they could. The war ended in humiliation. The South was left in ruins. In the chaos of Reconstruction, despair collided with the caste society, violence, and inequalities inherited from the earliest days of colonization.

The Lowcountry became a vast and desolate construction site. Since then, the territory has been reconfigured. In 1878, a new county appeared on the map, organized around a modest two-story red-brick courthouse. It was named Hampton County in homage to Wade Hampton, the Confederate general. A village of the same name grew up along the new railroad tracks. It consisted of a handful of streets and a few hundred residents who were attracted to this remote area by the promise of land priced lower than elsewhere.

After Reconstruction, Josiah Putnam Murdaugh established himself in Hampton. Before landing there, the Murdaughs had lived off phosphate mining, the fertilizer business, the sale of cotton, and various real estate transactions. They weren't rolling in money, but they were richer than their new neighbors. More respectable too.

Josiah Putnam Murdaugh II had the hard face of a bearded demon. He was a veteran of the War of Secession. He told whoever would listen that he had stood guard during General Robert E. Lee's surrender at Appomattox, guaranteeing him a place in history. His wife, Annie Marvin Davis Murdaugh, loved to introduce herself as a cousin of Jefferson Davis, the president of the Confederate States. A century and a half later, locals had their doubts about these prestigious bloodlines. Some even claimed that this was the Murdaughs' original lie.

In 1887, Josiah and Annie's fifth child was born: Randolph. He spent his first years surrounded by the pines, the swamps, and the sound of the locomotives. His legend was built on an anecdote. One day, Randolph saw a young man who was riding a freight train slip and get caught between train cars, and he pulled him to safety. The unfortunate man lost a leg in the accident, but the story held that Randolph had been the first to come to his aid.

At the dawn of the new century, Randolph was hungry to see other places. The young man hoped to wander the planet and live a life of adventure. He had dreams of enlisting in the Marines. We have little information about what followed, but we can imagine his journey. In the early twentieth century, a boy from the South bid farewell to his family and headed North, traveling up the East Coast. He showed up at the Naval Academy in Annapolis, Maryland, over five hundred miles from the town where he'd grown up and the only place he had ever known. Then, suddenly, everything fell apart. Doctors diagnosed him with a heart problem. He was declared unfit for any service and had to return home, back to the southern corner of South Carolina.

Upon his return, Randolph Murdaugh began executing his plan B: become a lawyer. He enrolled at the university, earned a law degree in 1910, and opened a small law office in Hampton. In the few photos of him still in existence today, Randolph Murdaugh, dressed in elegant gray suits, holds himself with pride, his hair neatly combed, his nose straight and expression serious.

Legend has it that he really didn't need to put up a sign on the storefront because obviously everyone knew who he was. Soon, Hampton and Murdaugh were synonymous. Randolph was everywhere. He was a school board member; a county delegate for the Democratic Party; the official lawyer of Varnville, the neighboring village; and a member of the various men's organizations with odd and complicated names in the area (Masons,

Chevaliers of Pythias, Woodmen of the World, Junior Order of United American Mechanics, Sigma Alpha Epsilon, Benevolent and Protective Order of Elks, etc.). In 1916, he founded a local newspaper. His network expanded. If you're going to live among the defeated, you might as well reign.

In most states, citizens vote every four years to elect a county prosecutor. This office is most widely called the district attorney, but in South Carolina, it is called circuit solicitor. As a legal representative of the country or district (made up of several counties), the circuit solicitor is responsible for undertaking legal proceedings in the name of the State and decides what will or will not be taken up in court to see that justice be done. The role of the district attorney or circuit solicitor is essential to the functioning of society. In a remote region where everyone knows one another, it is important to elect a person whom residents feel will fulfill the duties of his office.

In 1920, after declaring his candidacy at the office of the 14th circuit court, which covers five counties at the southern end of South Carolina, Randolph Murdaugh easily won the election for circuit solicitor. At the age of thirty-three, Randolph Murdaugh went after both the weak and the powerful, sued external auditors, bankers, a sheriff, and a pastor, and went after corruption. During murder trials, locals crowded the courthouse to see him present arguments like a formidable actor. He was reelected with no competition, then reelected again. Over the course of his terms in office, his name became synonymous with law and order.

Then, on July 19, 1940, death struck. Around one o'clock in the morning, a freight train was rolling through the darkness. Less than four miles outside Varnville, a machinist caught sight of a vehicle stopped before a railroad crossing. The driver of the car raised his hand as if waving to the engineer. The vehicle sat idling as the train approached. Then, suddenly, it jolted forward and stopped right on the tracks. The train collided with the car and, in an explosion of metal, dragged it three hundred yards down the tracks.

The body of the driver of the car was found sprawled on the ground near the railroad tracks, fifty yards from the crossing. Five days later, the *Hampton County Guardian* announced the news in banner headlines across page one: "Randolph Murdaugh Sr. Killed by Train." The funeral took place in Hampton. The county wept at the death of "one of its most respected citizens." Randolph Murdaugh Sr. left behind a family in mourning, as well as Murdaugh & Murdaugh, a law firm where one of his two sons practiced: Randolph Murdaugh Jr. The saga continued.

When asked to tell his life story, Randolph Murdaugh Jr. sometimes presented his existence as of the kind of story about overcoming odds that Americans adore. At the age of two, he lost his mother. As a small boy, he spent hours following Randolph Sr. around the corridors of the courthouse. He endured the crisis of 1929 when times were tough. Later, he went to college, thanks to no one but himself and his talents as a football player. In college, his feats established his reputation. During one football game, he "busted up" one of his opponents, earning himself the nickname "Buster" from his coach. After that, everyone started calling him Buster.

But that didn't keep him from having to work. During his college years, his days were scheduled down to the minute. Starting at seven o'clock every morning, he worked in the roads administration office; from 9:00 a.m. until 1:00 p.m., he attended classes and studied. From 3:00 to 6:00 p.m., he served as a law clerk in the South Carolina Senate. After graduating in 1938, he began working at his father's side as an assistant prosecutor.

When his father died in the train accident in the summer of 1940, Buster was twenty-five years old, with his whole life before him. He lost no time. On October 1, he went on the offense against the Charleston & Western Carolina Railway Co. for involuntary homicide. The personnel on board should have blown the whistle or rung the bell when approaching a railroad crossing, asserted the complaint. Furthermore, his father's view had been obscured by trees and bushes. The Murdaugh family sued for $100,000. On September 22, 1941, the two parties settled for an amount that was never disclosed.

In the years that followed, the Murdaugh family, led by Buster, continued suing the company, treating Randolph's accident like a judicial oil well to be pumped again and again. There were voices in town that expressed surprise. At the time of his death, Randolph Murdaugh had been up to his neck in financial trouble and his health had been in decline. He had just been released from the hospital. The night of his accident, he was on his way home from a poker party at the house of a friend. Was he thinking clearly? Was he in debt? Had things gone wrong? Could he have had himself killed?

Or wanted to commit suicide? Or make his suicide look like a murder, like Alex Murdaugh, eight decades later?

But these voices carried little weight around town. Buster was elected solicitor, like his father before him. Once, twice, three times. And like his father before him, he wove himself into the local canvas, serving as president of the Young Democrats of Hampton, member of the Social Protection Council, member of the executive committee of the County Democratic Party, founder of the Lawyers Association of South Carolina, and interim mayor of Varnville for two years . . .

Like his father before him, he hunted with police officers, fished with judges, played cards with lawyers, and mastered the art of asking people about the events in their lives, making them believe that they counted for more than others. Everyone was welcome to eat out of the hands of the Murdaughs. They entertained like the Gatsbys, and guests flocked to their barbecues and receptions. On one occasion, the *Hampton County Guardian* dedicated two entire columns to a party they hosted. The articled detailed the taffeta tablecloths and crystal candelabras. "The dining room table was the very idea of loveliness."

Buster attracted, charmed, and forged relations and soon made destinies. During a hunting party, he took a liking to the pastor, James P. Harrelson, and advised him to give the judiciary a try. He loaned him a few law books, and the pastor became a lawyer. After that, Buster helped him get started in politics, and the pastor ended up being elected senator.

At the Hampton County Courthouse, people could pick Buster out from a distance by the way he spit tobacco juice into a cup. He developed a reputation as a defender of the weak against the powerful, spiced up his arguments as a natural-born storyteller, and could transform an insignificant anecdote into an irresistible comedy.

In a letter dated May 21, 1951, a judge congratulated him on his "remarkable work" and his "rare sense of justice." Soon, people no longer called him "Buster" but "Handsome." Randolph Junior had surpassed Randolph Senior and was a more polished version of his father. Nothing but blue skies ahead. Until a scandal threatened to topple his impeccable success.

A fireball in the night. Federal agents had located a bootleg whisky distillery with a capacity of thirteen thousand gallons. On November 15, 1951, a raid was organized, shots exchanged, and the federal police dynamited the distillery. The investigation that followed brought to light what was known locally as "the whisky conspiracy," a vast network of illegal distilleries protected by the powerful in the region. Twenty-nine people were indicted, including a magistrate, a sheriff, and members of law enforcement—and Buster Murdaugh, who was scolded by the prosecutor for warning a bootlegger about the impending police raid, giving him time to move his production.

The trial opened on September 17, 1956. The questioning soon revealed that witnesses had been threatened or approached by the defendants and their lawyers and offered compensation in return for their silence. In fact, some of them retracted their statements on the stand. James P. Harrelson, the pastor and close friend of Buster, was one of the lawyers for the defense. A magistrate referred to a whole series of "friendly raids" orchestrated by the prosecutor. A former deputy sheriff confirmed having seen him pay the sheriff a $500 bribe in return for a light sentence for a bootlegger.

The Murdaugh system was brought to light. During the trial, another lawyer described him in this way: "He is a notch above the other defendants in intelligence. He didn't get caught in a distillery. He is too smart to have his fingerprints on the casks. The thirty-two distilleries that were implicated in this operation produced ninety thousand gallons of whisky during the period covered by the investigation. The conspiracy could not have existed without the knowledge and participation of the prosecutor." In other words, Murdaugh. The Murdaugh facade was cracking.

"Have you heard about efforts by the Hampton County Bar Association to disbar Murdaugh for lying to his clients and stealing from them?" asked a lawyer. The prosecution referred to him as the "mastermind, the brain, the man who'd led in the dance." The proof: he fished with the sheriff and hunted with a bootlegger.

Ten days into the trial, Buster Murdaugh took the stand. If he had to mount a defense, he would do it himself—and he would fight back. His name was all over the case? Payoffs? Just payment for investigations conducted by the sheriff in a civil case, that's all. The atmosphere grew tense.

In his conclusions, the prosecutor offered widely shared sentiments. "Jesse James rode a horse, but Mr. Murdaugh drives a Cadillac and has a law license." The district prosecutor said, "This man used to call himself 'Virtuous Randolph,' but now it's 'Bootlegging Buster.'"

Seventeen of those indicted were convicted, plus five others who had pled guilty after the trial started. Sheriff Thompson was sentenced to seven years in prison, one of his former deputies to four years, and a former magistrate to three. Oddly, Buster Murdaugh was acquitted. Later, it would come out that one of his cousins had met a jurist at a steak house in the area just a few days before the verdict.

In early 1957, Buster Murdaugh turned back to business. The world was beginning to change around him. It was the era of the civil rights movement. In a South haunted by the Ku Klux Klan, the ghosts of colonization, slavery, and the Civil War, the Murdaughs were on the right side of history. They were progressives as long as it served their name. They floated above the social divisions and got along with everyone—White and Black, rich and poor, powerful and vulnerable.

In the law firm, they were joined by others of like mind, attracted by power and influence. The storefront grew with the new arrivals. Murdaugh & Murdaugh became Murdaugh, Eltzroth & Peters, then Peters, Murdaugh, Parker, Eltzroth & Detrick (PMPED). Over the decades, the small family business became an empire.

Time had sculpted Buster Murdaugh's face. He had left his judicial problems behind. In the 1980s, he collected homages like a rock star on a never-ending tour. At a pig roast with seven hundred guests for ten dollars a plate, lawyers, judges, and police officers doffed their caps to him. A judge and childhood friend insisted that "no other lawyer can hold a candle to him." The president of the Beaufort County Bar Association declared that it would be "difficult to follow in Randolph's footsteps."

They served up anecdotes and unveiled a portrait of Buster, which had been painted by a local artist. This is the portrait that, for decades, would hang on the wall in the courtroom. In 1986, Buster was required by law to end his career. Thirty years after the great whisky conspiracy trial, Buster hung up his gloves and officially retired. He was seventy-two and had spent forty-eight years of his life serving the good people of the Lowcountry. His career had set the record for longevity in the history of the United States.

His son, Randolph III, would succeed him at the desk of the prosecutor. Born in 1939, a year before the first Randolph's death, the younger Randolph had joined the firm in 1964. His time had finally come. The years went by, and the Murdaughs still carried the day.

8

MURDAUGH, A USER'S MANUAL

In 1989, Hampton County had a bouquet of Randolphs. A photograph of three of them in front of the Hampton County Courthouse appeared on the cover of *Carolina Lawyer* (Today, *SC Lawyer*) magazine—the *Vanity Fair* of Southern attorneys. Pictured were Randolph II, Randolph III, and Randolph IV. Three suits, three serene smiles, and three confident gazes turned in the same direction. Inside the article, the three talked about one another. Randolph II brought in the legend of Randolph I, Randolph III sang praises to Randolph II, and the young Randolph IV listened to II and III and learned from them. "I don't think that any of us ever considered being anything but a lawyer," said one Randolph, doesn't matter which.

Economic liberalism triumphed in the 1990s. Multinationals flourished, and growth was steady. For the Murdaughs, business was going strong. Their secret? A judicial loophole. At the time, the law allowed residents of South Carolina to bring litigation in the county of their choice as long as the business in question had activity there. Say you lived in Columbia, two hours north of Hampton. During a trip, you slipped on a french fry in a McDonald's in Tennessee. You broke your arm and wanted to sue. If there was a McDonald's restaurant in Hampton County, you could register your complaint there and bring your suit against the fast food chain in Hampton County.

And if you knocked on the door at PMPED, you'd have a lawyer who fished with the judge, hunted with the jurors, and lunched with the whole county. Your chances of pocketing a jackpot increased significantly. Was that racketeering? In some ways, it was. Was it legal? Absolutely. In this country, where dragging people before a judge was a national sport, the ideal jurisdiction strategy even had a name: forum shopping.

Hampton was transformed into a place of pilgrimage for plaintiffs. The county became a forum where a certain America, an America of the past, of losers and outcasts, came to unstitch itself from the new America of globalization and uninhibited neoliberalism. There, an honest citizen could pick the pockets of a giant of capitalism with the blessing of the star-spangled banner.

CSX Transportation, a railroad company, was a target of predilection. Most often, accidents occurred elsewhere, but CSX freight trains trundled through the county. Between 1995 and 2002, the corporation paid out $18.8 million in verdicts and settlements in cases opposing CSX and PMPED. The PMPED offices grew to be one of the tallest buildings in the county. The edifice was nicknamed "the office that CSX built."

A note in passing: CSX was the descendant of the Charleston & Western Carolina Railway, the company implicated in the death of the first Randolph. Asking questions about whether personal vengeance played a role is not unreasonable. "A train killed my grandfather in 1940, and since then, they have continued to kill our community," declared Randolph III during a ceremony.

The lawyers in the firm were the best. Best of the best. At least, that's what they promised. The formidable Ronnie Crosby would rack up over 250 settlements worth over a million dollars each, including a few for over $10 million. The illustrious Johnny Parker appeared on lists of "Super Lawyers" of South Carolina and "The Best Lawyers in the United States," able to pull down $14 million in a single medical malpractice suit—an amount thirteen times the national average. The PMPED website listed an astonishing tally of the firm's multimillion-dollar victories, on behalf of the victims, against powerful entities such as Nissan, Ford, General Motors, Monsanto, and CVS. At one point, Walmart had considered opening a store in Hampton County but, in the end, decided not to. Too risky.

On February 5, 1998, Buster Murdaugh died at the age of eighty-three. The region mourned the loss of a "legend," a "larger-than-life personality," a man whose humanity was equaled only by his "encyclopedic knowledge of the law." Joking, the Beaufort County sheriff announced in the press that the law enforcement officers liked him so much that there would be no one on duty during the funeral. A Hilton Head attorney summed up sentiments. "The Lowcountry is a better place because Buster Murdaugh passed through there."

At that same moment, however, the rest of America was leaning forward to learn more about the strange case coming out of Hampton County and looking at it all a bit differently. In 2002, *Forbes Magazine* published an article titled "Home Advantage," which depicted an atmosphere from a bygone era, when the judge smoked in the courtroom, called the lawyers by their first name, offered them fresh-picked strawberries, and joined them for seafood at the local hangout right after presiding over a case with $13 million at stake. He shook hands with the local lawyer and blew a kiss to the defense attorney. At the turn of the twenty-first century, the county was suddenly becoming a symbol of an archaic, outmoded system of justice.

Another shock hit in 2004. This time, it was the American Tort Reform Association, an organization dedicated to judicial reform, that took on Hampton. The county was third on the list of "judicial hellholes," otherwise known as "magical jurisdictions." This is how Richard "Dickie" Scruggs, a Mississippi attorney defined them: "In these places, it is almost impossible to have a fair trial if you are on the side of the defense [...] Cases are not decided in the courtroom. They are won in the back room, long before they go to trial."

The portrait was damning, even worse than the article in *Forbes*. It pointed out that the number of complaints lodged at Hampton had doubled in the past five years and that most of the cases adjudicated in the county were brought by residents from other counties and other states. The cases concerning bodily harm damages had become an industry. The businesses related to the cases preferred settlements to trials because PMPED controlled the county. "Many out-of-town attorneys . . . are 'terrified' to have to come to Hampton County for a trial because of the unusually high verdicts and the number of plaintiffs' cases won in this County," said the report.

The firm suddenly looked like a two-story mafia. In 2005, a state law was passed to limit forum shopping. That cut into one of the firm's sources of revenue. A year later, Randolph Murdaugh III decided not to run for circuit solicitor. It would be up to the next generation of Murdaughs to demonstrate how to survive in this new world.

This story is a flashback to October 1973. A small five-year-old boy at the Hampton County Courthouse. With his little hand, he is reaching into a big jar to pull out the names of the next jurors, and this itself is an event. In a short, page-one article, the local newspaper introduced the public to the "fourth generation of Murdaughs at the courthouse." The child in question was the younger brother of Randolph IV, son of Randolph III, grandson of Buster and great-grandson of Randolph Senior. His name was Alex, but the newspaper messed up his name, writing "Alec."

At that time, the Murdaughs lived in a low, modern brick house in Varnville, the neighborhood favored by the county's lawyers, judges, and bankers. Despite their political power, "nobody drove a Mercedes," recalled James Tuten, who was their neighbor. "There was nothing ostentatious about their lifestyle."

Little Alex Murdaugh hung out with his pal, Russell Laffitte, who lived a few doors down the street. Together, they raised hell out in the pines. One day, they lit a fire. Another day, they broke a window by shooting it out with an air pistol. Alex's mother, Libby, a teacher, drove the neighborhood children to school. The Murdaughs didn't go to private schools but rather the public schools attended by the county's future citizens, elected officials, and jurors. "There was a certain racial and social diversity in our school," said James Tuten. "When you think about it, that was rare at the time."

Alex Murdaugh was not the most brilliant student at Wade Hampton High School. He was less intellectual than his older brother, Randy, and less of a troublemaker than his little brother, John Marvin. And yet, one day, Alex and James Tuten were called into the coach's office. "I think we were sleeping in class," Tuten recalled. The basketball coach decided to administer a severe hiding, three blows with a wooden paddle. James accepted his punishment, but not Alex. With his distinct twang, the Murdaugh boy pleaded his case. A lawyer was born.

In his teen years, James Tuten began to distrust Alex. He noticed that his childhood friend's behavior changed depending on the group he was with. One day, Alex came over to Tuten's house and played baseball. The next day, Alex acted tough to impress the guys. "I realized that he could be a manipulator," said Tuten. "He wasn't sincere, he wasn't authentic, he was conscious of his social status."

Alex was part of the popular crowd. He was tall and athletic and played basketball, baseball, and football. Like his grandfather before him, he played for the Red Devils, whose red jerseys paid tribute to the Red Shirts, paramilitary supremacist groups that had proliferated during Reconstruction in support of Confederate General Wade Hampton. Alex was a lineman on the football team. On the field, his job was blocking and tackling. "He was a good athlete," lawyer Jim Moss remembered. In a yearbook photo, he proudly wears the number 5, standing next to his girlfriend, Susie.

Alex liked girls, alcohol, and attention. In 1986, he was elected Wittiest, All-Around Best, and Most Athletic student. In his senior year, he was the king of self-promotion and especially party king. After the football games, the Murdaugh brothers liked to throw a big party in a field in Almeda, a few miles from Hampton. There, they would light a campfire, knock back a string of beers, and take turns disappearing into the back seats of their cars.

Alex's path had already been determined. After Wade Hampton High, Alex headed to the University of South Carolina. Like his ancestors, Alex played for the Gamecocks. At the university, he met future lawyers and friends, including a roommate named Cory Fleming. He joined Kappa Alpha, a social fraternity for wealthy, Southern young men, lovers of testosterone and clubbiness. At the age of twenty-one, he participated in the Old South Ball, a kind of reenactment costume ball event where young men dress in Confederate military uniforms and young women in hoop skirts like the ones in *Gone with the Wind*, soon to be eclipsed by modernity.

Also while in college, Alex fell in love with Margaret Kennedy Branstetter, the woman who would become his wife. Everyone called her Maggie. She was in the class behind his and was a sister in Kappa Delta. Born in 1968, a little farther north in Nashville, Maggie had been dragged around North Carolina, Pennsylvania, and South Carolina following her father's successive positions at Ford, IBM, and DuPont. Finally, after long years of moving about, the Branstetters settled down in Summerville, South Carolina, a small town sixty miles east of Hampton.

Maggie and Alex had no hesitations. They married in 1993 and already knew what their future would look like. "After a wedding trip to Jamaica, the couple will reside in Columbia," said the local newspaper. A few months before that, in February of the same year, Alex Murdaugh had been accused of starting a brawl in a strip club on Hilton Head Island. When things fell apart, he asked the police, "Do you know who I am?"

His undergraduate degree in political science was followed by law school and a law degree. Alex Murdaugh was never the most brilliant student in his class. That didn't matter; his name would take care of the rest. His first job was at a law firm in Beaufort. "His father called to ask me if I could take him so he'd be able to see what it was like before coming back to Hampton," said Jim Moss, who worked there at the time. "We took him on, and he did super work." Silence. "I don't understand what happened next."

Actually, it was pretty simple. Murdaugh had naturally gone back to the region where he'd been born, where his destiny called. Alex and Maggie had their first child in 1996. Richard Alexander Junior, like his father, and nicknamed Buster, like his grandfather. Then they had a second son, Paul.

Respecting tradition, Alex served with the solicitor on a volunteer basis and worked on certain cases with his father. And, as the family manual stipulated, he sent money to the Democratic Party—a lot of money, and under several different names. He was one of the biggest donors in the region. Then, once he had checked all the boxes, he joined the firm founded by his great-grandfather and embraced the adventure of cases involving bodily harm, work accidents, accidental falls, and defective tires. "He was good with people," said lawyer Ronnie Crosby. "He was good at reading people, very good at understanding people, very good at making them believe that he was interested in them and establishing a rapport of confidence."

In the Lowcountry, this latest generation of Murdaughs embodied a particular idea of modern happiness, a certain version of the American dream. They had a housekeeper, a gardener, and a whole fleet of pickup trucks, golf carts, and other vehicles to circulate on the property. They played golf and threw barbecues, as well as more formal evening affairs and parties for hunting deer, dove, or wild pig. They had another house at the shore in Edisto, which was valued at $920,000.

In one century, the lifestyle of the Murdaughs had transformed. Far from the asceticism of his ancestors, Alex spent more and more money on an increasingly ostentatious lifestyle. Some would have said that he had only adapted to the times. To attend the World Series in Nebraska, he took a small private plane with his old friends Cory Fleming and Chris Wilson. Occasionally, he flew off to Guatemala just to go fishing. For Christmas in 2016, he bought two .300 Blackout rifles for his sons for a total of $9,188. When Paul's Blackout went missing in 2017, he just bought him a new one. In 2018, it was Maggie's turn to receive a rifle costing $875. In 2021, Alex bought her a Mercedes for $85,000. After the murders, investigators found a Gucci receipt for $1,000. On weekends, the Murdaugh couple liked to take off on their fifteen-foot boat to go fishing and cruise on the river. Alex Murdaugh was the happy co-owner of seven private islands in Beaufort County.

However, as the 2020s approached, something was missing. Maggie was less and less present at the residence. She preferred to spend time at the house in Edisto. Soon the children would fly away from the nest. Alex Murdaugh was worried. One little hitch and everything could collapse.

9

THE LAST OF THE MURDAUGHS

One winter evening, after a daylong outing with friends in the Beaufort swamps a few miles from Hampton, Paul Murdaugh, the youngest of the clan, was ordering one last shot at a bar called Luther's, along with his friend Connor. Anthony and Mallory were outside, strolling along the edge of the water, looking at each other with young love. Miley and Morgan were on a swing on the porch of the bar, waiting for their respective boyfriends to finish. Finally, the two young men came out of the bar. Paul staggered along, lighting their way with a flashlight and waving his arms about incoherently. A few minutes later, the gang walked down a floating dock to their small boat and set out on the icy black creek. It was one o'clock in the morning on February 24, 2019.

Does a youthful error define a man? At only nineteen years of age, Paul already had a bad reputation in Hampton County. The townspeople thought Alex and Maggie Murdaugh's boys were poorly raised, spoiled rotten, maybe even dangerous. One woman called them monsters, little demons, terrorists. Or just the new generation of Murdaughs, the fifth, pushed to the level of white-hot.

The oldest, Buster, embraced the family path. He wanted to be a lawyer, be influential, and enjoy as much power as his elders. Law degree, fraternity, proud parents—for him, the line was straight. But for Paul, things were more complicated. He was not studious, had difficulty finishing whatever he started, and didn't seem to know what to do with his life. In a family where nobody needed to find themselves, failure was not an option. He found some comfort in Gloria Satterfield, the housekeeper, who was kind and attentive.

From his elders, Paul had inherited a taste for firearms, the outdoors, hunting, alcohol, partying, and the attention of others. His friends came over to have a good time on his island of Southern youthful pleasures.

Together, they guzzled beer, hunted game, and partied. The day Paul lost his semiautomatic, his father replaced it. At the Murdaugh house, everything was permitted. Especially alcohol. Paul drank a lot and often pushed limits. He drank beer through a funnel tube connected to an open can held above his head. He drank from glasses of all shapes and sizes. He jumped out of his boat, climbed electric poles, and lit fires. His friends liked to take videos of him on the verge of an alcoholic coma. They called this drunk and badly behaved version of Paul "Timmy"—the side of him that was detached from the weight of reality.

In high school, Paul met Morgan, and they fell in love. He was able to show tenderness and attentiveness to this young woman whose father was a landscape architect and mother an oncology nurse, and who exposed him to a different world. He gave her Valentine's Day gifts and invited her to go fishing in Guatemala and attend basketball games with his family. However, their relationship was complicated. They loved each other, then broke up, then loved again. A certain problem was always threatening. When Paul drank, he became aggressive. Run-ins with the authorities were increasing. Never anything serious, just small infractions.

Still, one evening in 2017, he lost control of his car on a curve in the road. He'd had too much to drink, and the vehicle flipped over with a trunk full of guns. Instead of calling 911, Paul called his grandfather, Randolph III, and then his father. The two arrived, cleaned up the car, and emptied the trunk of the rifles. No need to create a scandal.

After Gloria Satterfield's death in February 2018, things never settled down. Paul always kept a photo of her in his wallet.

During the day on February 23, 2019, before taking the boat out that evening, Paul stopped at Parker's gas station in Ridgeland, thirty miles south of Hampton. There, he bought Bud Natural Lights, shandies, cigarettes, and chewing gum. At the cash register, he used his brother Buster's ID and paid with his mother's credit card, then went off to join his friends.

They had all known one another since childhood. Miley, Morgan, and Mallory all worked in the same clothing store in Beaufort. Anthony and Connor were cousins. Anthony was going out with Mallory, Paul with Morgan, and Connor with Miley.

That afternoon, they got together in a house by the river that everyone called Murdaugh Island. Anthony and Mallory arrived a little later than the others. There, they drank their first beers and waited for sunset. Their destination: Paukie Island, where friends were having an oyster roast. To get there, the six friends took a little boat belonging to the Murdaughs. The girls sat on the ice chest, handing out beers to the boys. At around 7:00 p.m., they docked. The adults were there, even Paul's uncle, Randy Murdaugh. Everybody enjoyed oysters and beer.

At midnight, the teens decided to take off. Because they'd been drinking underage, they weren't sure they should call an Uber. Then Paul got into the boat. There was no way he was going to leave it there. And when Paul didn't want something, there was no point in arguing. The gang set off again. On the way, they had an idea: Why not knock back a few shots in a bar in Beaufort before getting back to Murdaugh Island? One last stop.

Paul and Connor went into the bar, each downing two lemon drops. Paul's hands clenched. Connor thought, "Timmy's back," as he watched his friend grow aggressive with some guys sitting at other tables. He flipped the empty chairs over as he walked past. In the end, it was time to leave; otherwise, the situation might get out of control.

Back on the boat, the headlight didn't work, so the friends took turns holding a flashlight as a replacement. Things grew tense. Paul was drunk, and Morgan called him out for it. Sometimes Paul would let go of the wheel, causing the boat to do donuts in the water. Connor sat next to the instrument panel and took over the controls just to straighten out their direction. Paul shoved Morgan, scaring Anthony and Mallory. Miley was shocked. "Stop it, Paul," they told him. They just wanted to go home. At about 2:20 a.m., the boat accelerated and collided with a piling of the bridge over the creek.

Three years later, while Alex Murdaugh's trial was in full swing, attorney Joe McCulloch kept himself busy in the pauses between statements by reading a book titled *The Last of the Bighams*, the true story of a massacre that had shocked South Carolina in the 1920s. In the preface, he had highlighted this sentence: "The family's fatal flaw, or so it seems to be, was a feeling of superiority that the Bighams bore toward the society in which they lived, the innate feeling that they lived above the judgment of those around them and that they were entitled to take whatever they were clever enough to seize." The Bighams fell apart in the 1920s. And the Murdaughs? His voice crooning, Joe McCulloch presented the fact as if it was obvious. "The moment when the boat collided with the bridge."

The trial stretched out like an endless day. A Chinese spy balloon had been shot out of the South Carolina sky, but other than that, it was Murdaugh, Murdaugh, Murdaugh all day, every day. On Valentine's Day evening, three men sat idly discussing the case after closing time at Coconut's. Five girlfriends discussed it during their wine tasting–club meeting, at which large glasses of vodka Gatorade were also served. In a house located at the edge of a golf course fairway, seated between a bookcase loaded with detective novels and a cat tree, Terry McLeod watched Court TV on an iPad hanging from a stool and wondered what everyone would talk about when it was all over.

Each morning, a convoy dropped Alex at the back of the courthouse, where weary photographers were waiting. John Monk injured his shoulder when he tripped over a television cable but just kept going. A wedding took place in the media space at the Wildlife Center, meaning the journalists had to be moved into the Reptile Room. A bomb threat (a real one) interrupted the trial, causing a quick evacuation of the courtroom. Two jurors caught COVID-19. Becky Hill caught COVID.

The Murdaugh family had to move back a row as punishment for attempting to pass a John Grisham novel up to Alex. Moreover, John Grisham himself was spotted in the courtroom. Except that, no, it wasn't actually John Grisham; it was Bill Young, the mayor of Walterboro.

A GoFundMe site was set up to help out a woman who was testifying against Murdaugh. Donations flooded in under pseudonyms like "Alex is guilty." To avoid losing his sanity, Scott Grooms sat in his office watching videos of the TGV, French superfast trains, rolling through the countryside in the south of France—so maybe it was too late, maybe he'd already lost it.

At noon, the little crowd headed for the food trucks. The restaurant owners had arrived at dawn. Shorty's Smokin' Butts cooked two hundred pounds of meat and served a hundred plates a day from their truck. For Edgar, the chef at Castillo's, the pizzeria located some three hundred yards from the courthouse, things were veering toward nightmare. The locals didn't want to come and be exposed to the circus, and the Yankees were slapping their money down on the counter of the food trucks. Edgar claimed to be losing $10,000 a day.

In the evening, tripods remained standing in front of the courthouse without photographers behind them.

Michael DeWitt wrote his article in his Ford pickup truck before taking off. The Court TV channel recorded a program at Fat Jack's, a steak house located across from Walmart, as servers sang "Happy Birthday" to a table of customers.

The day the Netflix documentary was released, Christie, an employee at the Colleton County Museum, organized a watch party at home with chili con carne and baked potatoes. Journalist Will Folks wrote his name on his red plastic party cup with a marker. The guests made themselves comfortable in the living room, with a scattering of children's toys on the floor. Back at the trial, one witness on the stand gave precise details on hunting wild pigs. As he stood facing the prosecutor with a rifle in his hands, defense lawyer Dick Harpootlian said, "Tempting." Among the crowd of visitors attending Alex Murdaugh's trial, some seemed to have come to verify things about themselves and the place where they had grown up. Amy Scheer had grown up in Hampton and said that until she left, she hadn't realized the degree to which corruption had sucked her city dry and impoverished the community. "It's good to see that times are changing," she said, standing in the courtroom. An old man had made the trip despite suffering from Parkinson's disease. Jamie Harrelson was the son of Senator James P. Harrelson, old Buster's best friend. He had known Randolph III well, and Alex after him. "He's a friend," he said. "Whether or not he is convicted, it won't change a thing, in my opinion." He also added that when he and Alex Murdaugh exchanged glances, the two men broke down in tears, as if hit hard by the weight of the past.

PART 4
THE ART OF BULLSHIT

10

MISCALCULATIONS

In April 2019, Paul Murdaugh was indicted for driving under the influence and causing the death of his friend Mallory Beach. He risked up to thirty years in prison but was not put in preventive custody. To save him from that, Alex paid the $50,000 bail and, not surprisingly, called on the services of the formidable Dick Harpootlian, who knew the judges better than anyone else.

Everything started as usual in the Lowcountry, except for one detail: this time, an innocent young woman had lost her life. And rumors circulating in the county predicted that the Murdaughs would not get out of this one so easily. Not this time. This drama had turned the tables. The newspapers turned their cameras on the case. Their finest investigators—Mandy Matney, Michael DeWitt, and John Monk—set to work.

In the street and on social media, Paul had been subjected to insults. Maggie, who felt uncomfortable, hardly ever left their second home in Edisto. As for Alex, he was dealing with a man named Mark Tinsley, a lawyer by trade and no stranger to fat courtroom files, who had decided to bring a suit against him as the owner of the boat. A relentless hunter who had decided to make Murdaugh his game, he was suing for $10 million.

As was his habit and as his elders had done before him, Alex tried to soften up this fellow attorney. At a lawyers conference, Alex took him aside and called him "Bo," a diminutive of "Bro" in the South. "What are these stories that I've been hearing, Bo? I thought we were friends."

Tinsley didn't budge. "We are friends. But if you think I can't set your house on fire and that I'm not going to give this my all, you are sadly mistaken. You are going to have to settle this case."

Alex dropped his guard. He didn't have $10 million. Tinsley pulled a face. Alex Murdaugh was a lawyer, and fate seemed to have smiled on him. He owned a seventeen-hundred-acre property and a house at the shore, and he had insurance. Of course he had $10 million. Time passed. Mark Tinsley came back to it but ran into a wall. Impossible to have the last word in this story. A hearing was finally scheduled, at which time Alex Murdaugh's finances would be exposed to daylight. The date was set for June 10, 2021.

The court date put the Murdaughs in a panic. Maggie confided to her new housekeeper that she didn't know how they were going to pay. They didn't have that kind of money and Alex wasn't telling her everything.

At the law firm, Annette Griswold, the paralegal, no longer acknowledged Alex. He was even more agitated than usual. Difficult to reach. Small financial anomalies caught her eye. In early 2021, Griswold noticed that $792,000 was missing from the accounts. She contacted the office of Chris Wilson, a lawyer who was one of Alex's best friends. The two men had worked together on a case for which the PMPED should have received the missing amount. The employee in Wilson's office indicated that the sum had already been paid in full to Mr. Murdaugh. That surprised Griswold. Fees were to be paid to the firm, not directly to the lawyer. That was procedure.

When Griswold asked Murdaugh, he told her that he had not received the money—there must have been some mistake. She pressed the issue, and he insisted. In late May, she referred the matter to the chief financial officer, Jeanne Seckinger, who had known Alex since high school. She had no doubt that he would provide an explanation. On June 7, she ran into him in the hallway at the firm. “What do you want now?” he asked her with an unusual look on his face. They stepped into his office, where he tried to reassure her. The phone interrupted their conversation. Alex Murdaugh’s father was in his final days. They would take care of this matter later.

A few hours after this aborted confrontation and three days before the hearing on the boating accident was to take place, Maggie and Paul were murdered.

After the murders, the boat accident hearing was canceled. Mark Tinsley even thought about abandoning the lawsuits. What would be the purpose of harassing a father whose wife and son had just been slaughtered? Beyond his own feelings, it was not a good judicial strategy. “In a civil suit, you have to motivate the jury to help one of the protagonists. If you have Attila the Hun attacking an adorable grandmother, who will come out of it with the best result? The grandmother.” Sympathetic people have the best verdicts; that’s just how it is. And it’s harder to seem more sympathetic than when your flesh and blood have just been murdered. At the firm, Alex’s colleagues also put the brakes on questions. Who would question the lawyer's probity at a time like this?

But the truce only lasted so long. Three years later, the team at the firm went to court. They had something to announce. The $792,000 was only the tip of the iceberg. After the period of mourning had ended, they had started digging again, they explained, and that was how they had discovered the truth concerning Alex Murdaugh. The truth? Jeanne Seckinger leaned forward, closer to the microphone. "I think Alex was successful more . . . not from his work ethic but for his ability to establish relationships and to manipulate people into settlements and clients into liking him. So, he did it through the art of bullshit, basically."

On September 2, 2021, a few months after the murders, everything became clear for the members of the PMPED law firm. That day, Annette Griswold was filing folders when a check floated through the air like a feather. It was signed by Alex Murdaugh, and the recipient was Forge. Suddenly, Griswold understood. Alex had lied to her.

To assure best practices to their clients, law firms call upon asset management companies, serious people who assess the financial situation of plaintiffs to structure the best possible settlements to optimize revenues over the long term. PMPED, as it happened, worked with an asset management company called Forge Consulting, LLC, based in Atlanta.

This was Alex Murdaugh's scheme: He had opened several accounts at the Bank of America under the name Forge. That's right: not Forge Consulting, just Forge. As a result, when Annette Griswold thought she was sending money to Forge Consulting, she was actually sending it to Forge—and therefore, to Alex. Alex Murdaugh had stolen money, a lot of money. How long had he been doing it?

The mid-2000s seemed to mark the turning point. The law limiting forum shopping, passed in 2005, had led to some difficulty for the Murdaughs. It meant fewer cases to plead and, therefore, less money. To compensate, Alex Murdaugh had started getting involved in real estate operations with a certain Barrett Boulware, a murky character whose name appeared in a dubious case of drug trafficking in 1983, involving the seizure of seventeen tons of marijuana from a shrimp boat off the coast of the Bahamas. Boulware was also the person from whom Alex later purchased the Moselle estate. The 2008 financial crisis struck the American economy at its heart, and the real estate market collapsed. For Alex Murdaugh, it was one more source of revenue that vanished. How could he replace the loss?

On August 22, 2009, a woman named Pamela Pinckney was driving down I-95 when she lost control of her vehicle. She survived with a few fractures, and her cousin was injured, but the situation was more serious for her son, Hakeem. His spinal cord was injured, making him a quadriplegic. The investigation showed that the accident had been caused by a defective tire.

At the hospital, Alex Murdaugh knocked on the door of Pamela Pinckney's room. He was an influential lawyer specializing in this type of case and inspired her confidence. The young Hakeem would need a conservator. Murdaugh suggested the name of a banker, Russell Laffitte, a childhood friend of his. To defend Pamela, Murdaugh suggested another lawyer, Cory Fleming.

On October 7, 2011, Alex Murdaugh obtained an out-of-court settlement with the tire company. The money arrived at the Palmetto State Bank, where Russell Laffitte was CEO. Four days later, the young Hakeem died at the hospital at the age of twenty-one. His respirator had been unplugged with no explanation. The Pinckney family never received the money that should have come to them—$1 million, according to her lawyer, Justin Bamberg.

A little earlier that same year, not far from Hampton in Allendale County, a UPS truck drifted sideways and collided with the car of Arthur Badger. His wife, Donna, died in the accident. Alex Murdaugh led the battle against UPS. The Badger family was supposed to receive $1.3 million but never saw a dime.

In 2015, a man named Deon Martin was injured in an automobile accident. Alex Murdaugh was accused of stealing more than $300,000 from him—by representing him, then depositing the settlement payment in his own Forge account.

In 2016, it was Manuel Santis-Cristiani. A victim of an accident, he hired Alex Murdaugh to represent him. Murdaugh sued and won a payment of $70,000. The money was supposed to pay for Santis-Cristiani's medical treatment but, in fact, it went straight into the Forge account. After that, Johnny Bush was injured in a car accident. The $95,000 that should have gone to him also ended up in the Forge account.

At that point, everything fell into place quickly. The dates, names, and amounts changed, but the scheme was the same. The $90,000 owed to the poor Jamian Risher? Forge. The $125,000 for police officer Thomas

Moore to cover medical costs for injuries sustained in a car accident? Forge. Again.

At the trial, it was now the hour of the spreadsheets. The prosecutor ran through Alex Murdaugh's alleged victims. Once again on the stand, Jeanne Seckinger recalled a memory from 2017. By accident, Alex Murdaugh had received a check for $120,000 that was intended for his brother, Randy. Later, Alex claimed to have lost the check, so a second check was made out for him to sign. In this way, he had been able, allegedly, to deposit this sum of money that wasn't his. Twice. In 2018, he performed this kind of sleight of hand with Jordan Jinks, a friend of the family—$85,000 the first time and $65,000 a bit later.

The year 2018 brought the strange death of Gloria Satterfield, the housekeeper who had worked for the Murdaughs for over twenty years. After the funeral, Alex suggested that the children of the deceased sue him for wrongful death so they'd be able to pocket an insurance payout from his homeowner's insurance policy. He recommended Cory Fleming, a trustworthy lawyer. Again Cory Fleming. That fall, the insurance paid top dollar at $505,000.

But instead of informing Gloria's children of the payout, Fleming told them the case was thorny and that, for everyone's good, it would be wiser to name an expert to handle the estate. A banker, for example. Maybe a guy who works in Hampton. Three streets and five hundred yards separated the PMPED law firm from the Palmetto State Bank. The two institutions did business in a two-step.

This time, the Satterfield case didn't fall into Russell Laffitte's lap but that of Chad Westendorf, vice president of the bank; however, he was not an expert in inheritance matters. Late in 2018, lawyer Cory Fleming and banker Chad Westendorf took their share of the honorariums on the $505,000. The rest went into Alex Murdaugh's Forge account.

On April 12, 2021, Murdaugh called Tony Satterfield, son of his former housekeeper. He couldn't promise to make them rich but did hope to obtain $100,000 for him and the same for his brother. That would already be a lot. Normally, this kind of scam would pass as easily as a letter through the US mail. But in the meantime, Paul's boat accident had occurred. And as journalist Mandy Matney was investigating Murdaugh, she had also discovered the $505,000 scam. When she informed Tony, he demanded an explanation from the lawyer. Alex assured him that things would work out. That was in June, less than a week before Maggie and Paul were murdered.

Twenty-four hours after his colleagues exposed the Forge loophole, they forced Alex Murdaugh to resign, on September 3, 2021. Alex said he was sorry and knew he would get caught in the end. A century after the first Randolph had established the law firm, the name was changed to Parker's Law Group. The name Murdaugh vanished as if it had never existed.

The following day, Chris Wilson paid a visit to his friend Alex at the home of Alex's parents. The two men had known each other since high school, when they played baseball together and were best friends—at least that's what Chris Wilson thought. But in truth, Alex Murdaugh had used Chris in his attempt to embezzle the $792,000 he owed the firm, stripping it of close to $192,000 in the process. When Wilson realized it, he asked Murdaugh to sign a promissory note acknowledging his debt of $192,000 to Chris Wilson. Alex did so.

On that day, as summer was waning, Wilson saw a wreck of a man standing before him. The fallen lawyer dissolved into tears and confessed his addiction to opioids. He said that was why he had deceived Wilson and all the others. He said he was sorry. Chris Wilson left. A few hours later, Alex Murdaugh called Curtis "Eddie"

Smith to try to orchestrate a suicide attempt disguised as murder.

In February 2023, looking shattered on the witness stand, Chris Wilson wept while describing this meeting on the precipice. "I considered him my best friend," he said. "And I believed that he thought the same of me." The prosecutor twisted the knife in the wound.

"And how do you feel now?"

"I don't know what I feel anymore, Mr. Waters."

Now it was Tony Satterfield's turn to take the stand. He was wearing a sweatshirt over a plaid shirt. He had a frail build, wore glasses, and had the thin face of a kid who'd never matured.

His lawyer, Eric Bland, gave him a hug the way a teammate reassures his fellow player who needs a little nerve for the penalty shot. Eric Bland specialized in litigation between colleagues. In September 2021, Tony had called on him to help recover the $505,000 owed to the Satterfield children. While investigating the case, Bland discovered that the $505,000 was not all the Satterfield children had been awarded. A supplemental civil liability policy had paid out $3.8 million. In all, Alex Murdaugh and his accomplices had embezzled $4.3 million.

"Had you given him permission to steal your money?" the prosecutor asked Tony Satterfield with feigned innocence.

"No."

"Why did you accept Alex Murdaugh's plan when he suggested that you sue him?"

"Because I trusted him."

Between lunch at a food truck and an interview in the little wooden cabin hastily erected by Court TV, Eric Bland laid out his understanding of the Gloria Satterfield case. Six months earlier, on June 3, 2022, the police had announced their plans to exhume the body of the former housekeeper. The family had granted permission. But Bland didn't think Murdaugh had killed her. "Why not? Because if you need to kill someone, you don't risk letting that person be taken away in an ambulance, where they might regain consciousness. On the other hand, I think that Alex Murdaugh exploited her death for his own financial gain."

What about Maggie and Paul? After considerable reflection, Judge Clifton Newman had decided to integrate the financial crimes into the trial, for they could constitute a motive for the murders. This was also the prosecutor's theory. For him, the explanation for this tragedy now had a source. With his back against the wall financially and feeling penned in on all sides, Alex Murdaugh could not tolerate the dishonor he was about to inflict on his prestigious lineage. Instead, he chose chaos. All that remained was to prove this theory.

11

ONE LAST BOMB FOR THE ROAD

Five weeks into the trial, a nonexhaustive list of the elements playing against Alex Murdaugh included:

- Three days after the murders, a hearing on the boat accident had been scheduled to take place, which would have revealed his spiraling debts, thefts, and lies.
- On the day of the murders, Alex Murdaugh had been confronted by the CFO of his law firm concerning $792,000 that Alex could not account for.
- Alex Murdaugh had texted Maggie, asking her to come home to Moselle for the evening.

- A few hours before the murders, a Snapchat video showed Alex Murdaugh in a polo shirt and khaki pants. However, when the police arrived at the scene, he was wearing a white T-shirt and khaki shorts, which would indicate that he had changed clothes.
- Alex Murdaugh was known for being on the phone all the time, but on the day of the murders, his phone registered no activity or movement between 8:09 p.m. and 9:02 p.m., the time frame during which the two murders were committed.
- The video recorded by Paul at the kennels located Alex Murdaugh at the scene of the crime only a few minutes before his wife's and son's estimated time of death.
- And if he hadn't committed them, how did he know he needed to lie about this particular point?
- At least one of the murder weapons was allegedly a gun belonging to the family.
- When the first responders arrived, Alex Murdaugh was clean from head to foot, even though he told them he had taken the

pulse of his wife and son, who were covered in blood.

- Three months after the murders, when he felt cornered again, Alex Murdaugh tried to fake his own murder—or attempted murder. It's not entirely clear which.

And if that wasn't enough, there were now questions surrounding Shelley Smith. She was Libby's caregiver—Libby, who was Alex's mother. Shelley explained to the court that after Randolph III died at the hospital on June 10, the eve of Maggie and Paul's funeral, she—Shelley—had had a strange conversation with Alex. On the night of the murders, he had come to the house to visit his mother. It was unusual to see him arrive at that hour. According to Shelley, Alex stayed for twenty minutes at the most. Alex estimated his stay at thirty or forty minutes. The caregiver knew very well that was false. Had Alex tried to convince her? If she needed anything, Alex assured her, he would be happy to lend a hand, even help her find a better job at the school. After all, he knew the principal well.

Like so many other witnesses in the trial, Shelley cried on the stand while telling the court all that. She seemed to be torn between loyalty and the truth.

"Did Alex stay for thirty or forty minutes?" lawyer John Meadors asked her.

"Not to my memory."

Silence. More sobs.

"Why are you crying?"

"Because it's a good family. I loved working there. I'm sorry that all this happened. These are good people."

"But he did not stay thirty or forty minutes?"

"No."

That's not all. One morning, just a few days after the murders, Alex Murdaugh again showed up at his parents' home—at 6:30 a.m., a time when he never came. He was carrying a mysterious blue tarp, which he took upstairs. In October 2021, in the same place, investigators found a big blue overcoat covered with gunshot residue.

Another surprising conversation came out. Two months after the murders in August 2021, a worried Alex went to speak to Blanca, the new housekeeper. He seemed preoccupied. The police had shown him a Snapchat video that had been filmed just a few hours before the murders and in which he appeared wearing a shirt, he said. A Vineyard brand dress shirt, he specified. That was important. But it wasn't a dress shirt; it was a polo shirt. Blanca knew for sure because, on the morning in question, she had fixed his collar.

What else? After the murders, water was running from the garden hose at the kennel, but the gardener said the hose was not arranged the way he'd left it. He knew what he was talking about; this was his profession. In addition, gunshot residue had been found on Alex Murdaugh's clothes and on the seat belt in his Chevrolet Suburban.

There was one last bombshell concerning Alex's movements. Thanks to new GPS data just transmitted by General Motors, SLED Special Agent Peter Rudofski could now write out a complete timeline of the evening of June 7, 2021.

It started at 9:00 p.m., an unusual time for movement to begin. From 9:02 to 9:06 p.m., the number of steps taken by Alex Murdaugh increased significantly. He took 283 steps in the space of four minutes, which meant more than one step per second, immediately after the estimated times of the murders. He was in movement and, from that point, moving increasingly quickly.

At 9:07 p.m., Alex Murdaugh set off in the car to visit his mother in Almeda. After passing the place where Maggie's phone would be found the next day, Alex's car accelerated, reaching sixty-six miles an hour—fast even for daytime travel–while sending and making phone calls.

At 9:22 p.m., Alex arrived at Almeda. Interesting detail: a few seconds after turning into the lane, the car drove onto the grass not far from the woods, and the driver parked behind the house. Was Alex Murdaugh taking advantage of this gap in time to hide the weapons until he could come back later to dispose of them for good?

At 9:43 p.m., twenty minutes after his arrival—not forty, as he claimed—he took off in the direction of Moselle. On his return trip, the car moved even faster, reaching eighty miles an hour at 9:51 p.m. on a country road after dark.

"Would you drive, or have you ever driven, at a speed of eighty miles an hour with the rotating lights on?" Prosecutor Creighton Waters asked Special Agent Peter Rudofski. "No."

"Explain why to the jury."

"Because of the time of day, because of the density of wild animals that roam at that time of day—deer cross there all the time. And because of the road, which is full of potholes."

At 10:00 p.m., Alex Murdaugh arrived at Moselle. Five minutes later, he came out of the house, going toward the kennels. Barely twenty seconds after he'd parked his car, he dialed 911. Nineteen seconds to discover the massacre, go over to the bodies of Maggie and Paul, take in the horror that had just struck, and call emergency services. That's not much time.

To conclude, the prosecution presented photos of the happy family alongside the last texts sent. A few weeks before, on May 6, 2021, Paul had sent Alex a message that no one would want to send. "I'm still at EB [Edisto Beach] because we need to have a talk with you here. Mom found packets of pills in your computer bag." The next day, Alex texted Maggie, "I'm really sorry to do this to you. I love you." Mother and son only had one month to live.

Buster Murdaugh, aged twenty-six, came to the stand. He had his father's pink complexion, and his red hair was combed into a wave. He told his story in a voice devoid of emotion. At 9:10 p.m. on the evening the murders were committed, he received a phone call from his father, which lasted one minute. Everything seemed fine. A little later, he called again. "He asked me if I was sitting down, then told me that my mother and brother had been shot." That's all.

Was there any violence in the family? No. As far as his father's addiction, Buster knew. At least a little. When the court showed the video of Alex Murdaugh's birthday, filmed a few days before the murders, Jim Griffin encountered Buster's same impassive, disillusioned facade.

"What is the date of your father's birthday?"

"Umm . . ."

"This is not a test. You can tell us if you don't know."

"I don't know the exact date. Maybe the twenty-seventh."

He glanced over at Alex. Buster's mouth was half-open. He looked haggard and a little groggy. For a long time, he'd wanted to be a good Murdaugh. He'd checked all the boxes, even the ones for lying. That day, on the stand, he looked stunned, as if this nightmare had been going on for too long.

12

ALEX'S DAY

On the morning of the twenty-third day of the trial, thunder rumbled through the southern part of South Carolina. Alex Murdaugh was getting ready to testify. His lawyers did not seem thrilled. The judge asked him to rise. When he stood, he was taller than everyone else.

"Mr. Murdaugh?"

"Yes, sir. Morning."

Clifton Newman explained the Fifth Amendment of the Constitution, which authorized the defendant to refuse to testify against himself. He was not required to speak, and the final decision to speak was his alone.

"Do you have any questions?"

"No, sir. Thank you."

"Have you made your decision?"

"Yes, sir."

"And what is your decision?"

"I am going to testify. I want to testify."

He had listened, and now it was his turn to speak.

"Careful, watch the step," said Becky.

Seven decades earlier, Becky's grandfather had been among the defendants in the Colleton County whisky conspiracy in which the old Buster Murdaugh had been involved.

On that day, February 23, 2023, the clerk stared hard at the defendant and made him swear to tell the truth, the whole truth, and nothing but the truth. He sat down, adjusted the microphone, and spelled his name with a slight smile as if everybody didn't already know. "M-U-R-D-A-U-G-H." With a nod, he greeted the jurors one by one and offered them the face of an ordinary man, a mirror of themselves. "Morning," he said in an amicable voice.

His lawyer acted like he was attacking him. "Mr. Murdaugh, did you take this gun or any gun like it and blow your son's brains out?"

"No. I did not."

The lawyer asked if he had shot Paul in the chest or shot Maggie with an automatic rifle. To each question, Alex Murdaugh delivered the identical firm response:

"No." It was like a poorly rehearsed play. Sitting at an angle, almost turned toward the jurors, Alex looked them straight in the eye. He knew that all he had to do was sow doubt in the mind of one of the jurors, any one of them, at any time. So he repeated, "I did not shoot my wife or my son. Any time, ever."

On the other hand, he had come to confess one thing. On the evening of the murders, he had been present at the kennels with Maggie and Paul. For the first time since June 7, 2021, Alex Murdaugh confessed to lying.

Here were the facts as he was now telling them. On Friday the fourth, three days before the murders, Alex Murdaugh had spent the night at the hospital at his father's bedside. He'd slept in a chair. The next day, on Saturday the fifth, Alex, Maggie, and Buster had all met in Columbia to help at a regional baseball tournament. On Sunday the sixth, Alex and Maggie had gone to see another game before going home to Moselle. They visited Alex's ailing parents and took them a box of Krispy Kreme donuts. On the seventh, they woke up at Moselle. Concerning what followed, he intended to persuade everyone that, apart from the murders, it was an ordinary Monday.

On the morning of June 7, 2021, Maggie left Moselle for a doctor's appointment in Charleston. From there, she went to their second house in Edisto. At work, Jeanne Seckinger had, in fact, confronted Alex Murdaugh about the missing money, but it was nothing alarming, he'd assured her.

"Did you worry that your house of cards was about to fall?" interrupted Jim Griffin.

"On June seventh? Absolutely not."

And the hearing on the boat accident, planned for June 10, 2021, which would presumably reveal his financial situation?

"I had been a lawyer all my life. I did exactly the same thing as Mark Tinsley. After practicing for twenty-seven years, I knew that the plaintiffs always try to obtain documents for the defendant. I had never seen a judge order more than a statement of net worth."

Back home from work at the end of the day, he joined Paw-Paw.

"Who's Paw-Paw?" asked Jim Griffin, surprised.

"Paul, my son Paw-Paw, Paul Murdaugh," he answered, surprised by the question. "I called him Paw-Paw, Maggie called him Paw-Paw, Buster called him Paw-Paw, lots of people called him Paw-Paw."

Yet this was the first time during the trial that anyone had used this nickname. Alex Murdaugh offered a lot of details—on the different parcels of the property, on the

Labradors and their personalities, on all kinds of things that had very little to do with the murders but which he was proud to talk about. So, Alex and Paul had taken the tour of Moselle in a black pickup truck. They'd checked on the sunflowers. Tears came to his eyes.

"You were having a good time together?"

"You couldn't be with Paul and not have a good time."

When Maggie arrived, Alex came back to the house. He was sweaty, so he went to take a shower, then put on a white T-shirt and khaki shorts. After dinner, Maggie wanted to go down to the kennels and asked him to come along. He had just washed, so he didn't really want to go back out into the heat with the dogs. But then, well, okay. "Often, when Maggie asked me to do something that I didn't want to do, I changed my mind and decided to go." He climbed into a golf cart and drove to the kennel. The Labradors were running after guinea fowl. Bubba had caught a chicken, so Alex inserted his thumb in the dog's mouth to loosen its jaw and free the bird. And after that?

"I left. I went back to the house where it was air-conditioned." That was it.

Afterward, he lay down on the couch and took a nap. Or maybe not—he wasn't actually sure anymore. What he did remember, on the other hand, was that he decided to visit his mother, who had advanced Alzheimer's. Before leaving, he tried to call Maggie and sent her some texts. He received no response. "I wasn't worried," he said. One, Maggie was with Paul. Two, reception was bad at Moselle. So he set out, without going past the kennel.

He parked behind his parents' house, as always, because his mother's bedroom was on that side. He knocked on the door, but the caretaker, Shelley Smith, didn't hear, so he called her so she could open the door for him. "My mother was awake, I held her hand," he said. She wasn't doing well at that moment." It was sad to see her that way, and it was probably why Maggie hadn't gone along. The minute-long stop at the side of his parents' house? "I was getting my telephone. It had fallen down between the armrest and the seat."

"Were you hiding the weapons used in the crimes, Alex?"

"No."

"Were you hiding bloody clothes?"

"No."

Twenty minutes after his arrival—by now, it was clear that he had not spent thirty to forty minutes there—Alex returned to Moselle. He drove toward the house. The lights and the television were on, but

Maggie and Paul were not there. "I wasn't surprised," he said, "but I thought they'd come back in." After a few minutes, he decided to go out to see if they were down at the kennel.

"What did you see?"

"I saw what you saw in the photos."

A thread of mucus dribbled from his nose. His voice broke. After a thick silence, he said, "So bad."

The bodies, the panic, the horror . . . everything happened so fast. In twenty short seconds, he jumped out of his car, realized what had happened, and dialed 911. He took Maggie's and Paul's pulse while on the phone, he said. When the lawyer asked him why he tried to turn his son's body over, Alex murmured, "I don't know, I don't know. I don't know why I tried to turn him over. He was lying there, his face to the ground, I saw his brain on the ground. I didn't know what to do." Tears came to his eyes again.

If the story was as he told it, why lie about being at the kennel? Three times he'd lied: the evening of the murders in Agent Owen's car, during the interrogation three days later, and finally, two months after the double murder. To understand that, Alex countered, they had to understand the demon that had been chasing him for a long time: oxycodone. His addiction had started in the early 2000s after a knee operation related to an old football injury. His consumption of the pills had increased over time. Always more.

In December 2017, he entered rehab for the first time. Later, he returned to rehab one or two more times . . . he kept falling back into it. "Withdrawal from opiates is . . . wow, it's hard," he summed it up for the jury, his tone pedagogical. "First, you're sick. You vomit. You have terrible diarrhea. You perspire like you've just run a marathon."

On the evening of June 7, 2021, because of the drug, he was unable to reason in a sensible way. Agent Owen's questions about his relationship with Maggie and Paul paralyzed him. He had paranoid thoughts. So, he lied, and today, he regretted it. "Once I'd lied, I had to keep lying," he explained. As he was explaining himself in court, Alex Murdaugh had been sober for 535 days. "And I'm very proud of it."

"Did you love Paul?"

"Did I love him? Like nobody else. Him and Buster."

"Did you love Maggie?"

"More than anything else. I loved Maggie from the first time we met."

"Did you kill Maggie?"

"I would never hurt Maggie. I would never hurt Paul. Never. Whatever the circumstances."

It was coming up on four o'clock. Murdaugh stared at prosecutor Waters, who stared back.

"Mr. Murdaugh, let's begin with the things on which we agree."

A little family history. Randolph Murdaugh Sr., the old Buster, and Randolph III.

"An unbroken chain of prosecutors, correct?"

"Correct."

The defendant had known his grandfather, who'd served as a prosecutor for forty-six years. He loved him.

"He was your idol, wasn't he?"

"Yes."

The prosecutor took his time, leaning on the desk, delivering his summary with a certain pleasure.

"You started with Moss & Kuhn, then you went into the firm that had opened in 1910 but no longer exists because of your activities, correct?"

"Correct."

"Let me remind you," Creighton Waters warned. "The defendant is a former lawyer specializing in cases of bodily harm. That means two things. The first is that he made his career by dissecting his clients' vehicle and cell phone data. That is his area of expertise. The second is that he is a master in the art of persuasion, in reading others and modulating his speech to achieve his ends.

Have you called your son Paw-Paw previously during this investigation?"

"I don't know."

Don't be duped, the prosecutor seemed to say pointedly. The jurors were attentive.

On the second day of testimony, Creighton Waters had another lie to expose. Yesterday, Alex Murdaugh had said under oath and before the court that on the eve of the murders, he'd been at a baseball tournament with the family. The prosecutor presented the texts exchanged with Maggie. Alex had remained in his hotel room until late that morning. He was suffering from oxycodone withdrawal. In his testimony, he had omitted any mention of this.

After this warm-up, the prosecutor wanted to examine the details of what he called the defendant's "new story." According to this story, Alex had then taken the golf cart to go find Maggie and Paul. Bubba had a chicken in his mouth. In the video, recorded at 8:44 p.m., Paul filmed Cash in his cage. Referring to Bubba, Maggie said, "He has a bird in his mouth."

Alex called, "Come here, Bubba!"

And then? "I must have taken the chicken out of Bubba's mouth ten or fifteen seconds after Maggie said that." He then walked some three yards to set the chicken down on the ground. Altogether, he said that he'd spent about two minutes there.

"It was 8:46 p.m.," the prosecutor said, clarifying. "And after that?"

"I left."

"Yesterday, you said you ran out of there. Why did you leave so quickly, Mr. Murdaugh?"

"Because it was chaotic. It was hot. I was doing exactly what I didn't want to be doing."

"You were doing what you didn't want to do?"

"Correct. I was getting all sweaty."

"Did you say goodbye in your new version of the story?"

"Did I say goodbye?"

He'd probably said something like that, but he couldn't remember the exact words. He did not recall the last words he ever said to his wife and his son, and that didn't seem to haunt him.

"You have a rather photographic memory of this new story, so what happened?" Let's review. He took the golf cart, drove to the kennel, took the chicken out of Bubba's mouth, then disappeared at top speed because it was too hot outside. "Does that sound like real life?" asked Creighton Waters.

Murdaugh dodged the issue.

According to "the new story," the prosecutor continued, Alex Murdaugh had returned to the house at 8:49 p.m., at which time Maggie and Paul's phones were locked forever. Next, he allegedly stretched out on the couch for "the shortest nap in the history of the South." After about an hour or so of inactivity, his telephone was activated at 9:02 p.m. Between 9:02 p.m. and 9:06 p.m., it recorded hundreds of steps, more than at any other time that day.

"What were you doing?"

"I was getting ready to visit my mother."

"You were getting ready? I thought you'd already taken a shower. What did you need to do to get ready?"

"I can't tell you exactly what I was doing."

"Were you working out on the treadmill? Doing jumping jacks?"

He didn't know what he was doing, but he knew what he was not doing. "Washing. Cleaning the weapons. Cleaning a coat."

"The real reason for these steps, Mr. Murdaugh, it is that you were up at 9:02, moving around, then calling people to manufacture an alibi for yourself, isn't that true?"

"That is absolutely false."

If Alex had had nothing to do with the murders, then who would be implicated? Murdaugh had insisted from the beginning that, for him, the horror had struck because of the boat accident. "I never, never, never thought that the kids who were in the boat or their parents or their families . . . had anything to do with Maggie and Paul," he said today, however.

It was difficult to follow. "What you're saying to this jury," said the prosecutor, trying to interpret, "is that we're talking about random killers who knew that Maggie and Paul would be at Moselle on June seventh, who knew that they would be alone at the kennel on June seventh, who knew that you wouldn't be there, but only between 8:49 and 9:02, that they would have arrived without arms on the assumption that they would find rifles and ammunition on the property, that they would have committed the crimes in this short period of time, and that afterward, they would have left taking the same direction as you, for Almeda. Is that what you are saying to the jury?"

"You have a lot of factors in there, Mr. Waters. I don't agree with everything."

If he'd had nothing to do with the murders, how could he know he would need to lie on this particular aspect of the case? And when did he decide to lie about his presence at the kennel, exactly? He'd started doing it the night of the murders. The SLED agents took his fingerprints. During the first interview in the police car with Agent Owen, the questions about his relationship with Maggie and Paul had scared him. The paranoia had sucked him in. That's what he'd said yesterday, and he'd said it again today.

Forehead creased, the defendant followed the prosecutor with his eyes as he paced left and right.

"When responsibilities knock at the door, bad things happen, isn't that true?"

"What do you mean by 'bad things'?"

"June seventh happened. September fourth happened."

"I don't think June seventh happened because responsibilities were knocking at the door."

"For the first time in your life of privilege, influence, and wealth, as you were staring at your responsibilities, you suddenly became a victim, and everybody ran to your rescue. Is that not true?"

"I don't agree."

"For you, shame is an extraordinary provocation, isn't it, Mr. Murdaugh?"

Silence fell over the courtroom, and then the prosecutor asked a question about a certain category of criminals.

"Mr. Murdaugh, are you a family annihilator?"

"Do you mean, did I kill my wife and my son? No."

Furthermore, he never would have hurt them. For several minutes, the prosecutor asked him if he had lied to Maggie, to Paul, to his father Randolph III, to his brothers Randy and John Marvin, to his best friend Chris Wilson, to his associates in the firm Jeanne Seckinger and Annette Griswold, to his clients Pamela Pinckney, Hakeem Pinckney, Manuel Santis-Cristiani, Arthur Badger, and Deon Martin. He had lied to the police officers on the incident at the side of the road too.

"Do you know why people lie, Mr. Murdaugh? Because they know they have done something bad."

For over ten years he's been lying like he breathes. And now, we're supposed to believe his new story? One last thing. The prosecutor walked over to the computer. The video filmed by Sergeant Daniel Greene's body camera appeared again. He hit Play.

"They're dead, is that it?"

"Yes, sir, that's what it looks like."

"When did you see them for the last time? Or when did you talk to them for the last time?"

"Uh . . . earlier in the evening. I don't remember the exact time, I left for my mother's house for maybe an hour and a half, and I saw them forty-five minutes before that."

Pause.

A bald-faced lie. That didn't fit. Alex Murdaugh had been at the kennel and therefore saw them about fifteen minutes before leaving. The SLED agents had not yet arrived, nobody had yet lifted his fingerprints, and he had not yet had his crisis of paranoia. But he was already lying.

"All these explanations that you have just given the jury are the most important part of your testimony, and it was a lie, once again. Right, Mr. Murdaugh?"

"I don't agree."

"I have nothing more to add."

Three things the people assembled in the courtroom now knew about Alex Murdaugh:

1. He was a thief. He had robbed those who had the misfortune to gravitate to him. The most unfortunate, Whites and Blacks, the healthy and the disabled, the strong and the weak, perfect strangers, and those closest to him.
2. He was a liar. He had lied to a mass of people, especially about key elements of the case, claiming that he had not been in the kennels with Maggie and Paul, even

though a video located him there a few minutes before the murders.

3. He was a man who was falling. The last offspring of a powerful family, an opioid addict who had locked himself in a downward spiral of thefts and lies that were about to be unveiled for everyone to see.

Pollen covered the vehicles parked in the Hampton streets, and Alex Murdaugh had just buried himself alive.

PART 5
AFTER THE STORM

13

VERDICT DAY

Twenty months had passed since the murders, and a convoy was on the road toward Moselle. Three vans took the jury to the scene of the crimes. The cars headed toward this gray and green place at the end of the world. Judge Newman drove with Captain Jason Chapman, who had been one of the first to arrive on the premises on June 7, 2021.

At 10:07 a.m., Dick Harpootlian's black Mercedes arrived. A handful of journalists and photographers who had made the trip set up tripods and a stepladder. A *New York Post* photographer was wearing a beige hat. Young local reporters Ted and Thad took notes. Only the journalist Valerie Bauerlein of the *Wall Street Journal* was given permission to visit the crime scene after the jury was finished. Her name had been pulled out of the hat. Sitting in the back of a pickup truck, she was now typing up what she had seen for all her colleagues.

The sky was overcast, birds were singing in the trees, roadkill was decomposing at the side of the road, and the wind lifted its odor of death. A NO TRESPASSING sign by the low brick wall prohibited access to the haunted estate. Curious people sometimes came by to take photos. Drones flew over the zone, recording footage for documentaries and YouTube views. The grass had grown and the bushes needed to be pruned. A deflated football lay on the ground.

There were no dogs at the kennel anymore. There was still a gunshot hole in a window. Visitors had no trouble imagining the scene. For almost six weeks, they'd heard from more than seventy witnesses—friends, police officers, experts, and specialists, including forensics pathologist Ellen Riemer and crime scenes expert Kenneth Kinsey. Together, they had reconstructed everything in detail.

On June 7, 2021, when the first gunshot went off, Paul Murdaugh was right there, inside the four-by-six supply room. His wounds indicated that he had not defended himself. The prosecution deduced that he knew his murderer and had been taken by surprise. Most likely, he was standing to the side, possibly in a corner perpendicular to the door and to the shooter. If he had been facing him, he would have been killed immediately. However, Paul did not die right away.

Seriously wounded, he made his way toward the door. Slowly. The second shot came from his left when he was outside, right near the doorframe. The gun barrel was about three feet away from him, held low but aimed upward at a 135-degree angle. The impact took the shape of a cone. The bullets traversed the shoulder and the neck before reaching the head and coming out the top of his skull.

Twelve steps, or about nine yards, away, Maggie had fallen to the ground. Her wounds indicated the impact of at least five bullets from at least four gunshots. The angles at which the bullets had hit indicated that they had been shot very quickly from a distance of about three feet. She had been moving at the time. After a bullet hit her in the abdomen, Maggie allegedly fell forward onto her hands and knees. A first shot to the head finished her off, followed by a second. The scene indicated a certain disorganization. On the stand, Dr. Kinsey insisted forcefully on one point. "I cannot include or exclude two shooters."

Everyone was back in the courtroom. It was time for closing statements. Creighton Waters, the prosecutor, told the story like a tale. A tale of a being in a downward spiral. A man about fifty years old, from an influential family, enjoying a life of privilege but carrying a too-weighty past on his shoulders, in a life governed by a certain idea of success, power, and what it means to be a man.

"He was living a lie," Waters stressed. For a long time, nobody knew who he was. Slides paraded by in the PowerPoint, illustrated with photos, playing on the screen. Had Alex Murdaugh betrayed his clients? A photo of a fist. A storm was going to let loose on the Murdaughs? A photo of a storm. After the boat accident, the situation became unbearable. Alex's world collapsed; his ego couldn't accept it. "And he turned into a family annihilator."

The video at the kennel, the weapons, the timeline. Only one person had the motive, the means, and the opportunity to commit these murders. Waters ended with "Don't be taken in."

In his closing statement, Jim Griffin once again pointed out the gray areas in the investigation. John Meadors, the lawyer who looked like Lieutenant Columbo, had the last word. He made a point of thanking the dogs. Without Cash, there would not have been the video at the kennel. And without Bubba, no chicken, and no Alex Murdaugh in the video. "I think he loved Maggie and Paul," he continued. But if there was one thing to know about Alex Murdaugh, it was that he loved Alex Murdaugh above all else.

That evening, everyone headed for the media space at the Wildlife Center. To celebrate the last days of the trial, the clerk of court, Becky Hill, had planned a kind of concluding banquet. Her daughter, Aubrey, a country singer whose first album, *Shine*, had just come out, showed up to give a concert. Shorty's Smokin' Butts had prepared pulled pork and little ramekins of mac 'n' cheese for the occasion. A local journalist was drinking vodka and cranberry juice. Joe McCulloch gave a little speech. The food and alcohol were for him. Why? "Because I'm a nice guy," he said, grinning. "Except when I come after you in court."

Aubrey sang *Stand by Me*. Becky Hill danced with her husband. Everyone seemed to be having a good time. Alone in the Reptile Room, John Monk continued to write. A reporter was surprised by this atmosphere and wondered, was there any lesson to be taken from this case?

While awaiting the verdict, one celebrity gave his opinion. From afar, O. J. Simpson offered his views on the court spectacle, offering a prognostication. "The Juice" predicted that if the verdict came soon, Murdaugh would be declared guilty; if the deliberations took longer, he might get off with a hung jury. "Lying and stealing are different than killing." The football player accused of killing his ex-wife and one of her friends in 1994 had not watched the whole trial, but when you got right down to it, he was thinking, "It would not surprise me if this guy won the case."

Then the signal—the real one—came at the end of the twenty-eighth day of the trial. Defense lawyer Phillip Barber, looking downcast, was sitting at the counter in the Main Street Grille, drinking beer and eating chicken wings. He was talking to Brooke Brunson, the producer of the HBO documentary on the Murdaugh dynasty, when a guy tapped him on the shoulder and said, "We have to go."

At the same moment, reporters in the Wildlife Center media space saw movement on the live stream and jumped out of their chairs to rush to the courthouse. Others had figured it out when they saw Nancy Grace's makeup artist set up her equipment. Christie said that she'd been in the restaurant, paid her check quickly, and urged her husband to pass a car right in town so she'd get there in time. It was 6:41 p.m., March 2, 2023, three hours after deliberations had begun. The single word that had brought journalists, lawyers, and the curious flocking to the courthouse was "verdict."

The atmosphere was electric. James From Court was in place. A security officer asked for silence. The first hint of applause and they'd all be out the door. It was 7:00 p.m. Judge Newman made his entrance into the courtroom and asked that the jury be brought in.

"Do you have a verdict?"

"Yes, sir."

Alex Murdaugh rose. In an impersonal voice, Becky Hill read the charges. For each one, the same verdict was delivered: "Guilty."

As the defendant's fate was sealed, he blinked and lowered his head but remained standing straight. On the bench behind him, Buster leaned on the armrest. He wiped his red face, redder than usual, but he remained impassive.

"Proof of guilt is overwhelming," added the judge. The next day, he would pronounce the sentence. The silence was broken only by the sound of handcuffs. With his hands bound, the convicted man disappeared through a door. The family was escorted out by the police.

The floodlights outside the courthouse lit up the night. The prosecution team was exultant, hugging one another. So were the investigators. The journalists were active on the courthouse lawn. Becky Hill smiled from the balcony. People congratulated one another, and it felt like victory night at the World Cup finals.

A journalist from the *Guardian* in England had been dropped in on an emergency basis. Arriving exactly six weeks late, he seemed a little lost and was asking who was who. Scott Grooms prepared the bouquet of microphones at the podium. Facing a wall of video cameras, Prosecutor Creighton Waters declared that, finally, justice had been done. He had one last moral lesson to serve up: “It doesn’t matter who your family is. Doesn’t matter how much money you have or how much people think you have. Doesn’t matter how influential you are. If you break the law, if you kill, justice will be done in South Carolina.”

The next morning, the convoy parked behind the courthouse. Like the first day of the trial, the van door opened, and the murderer climbed out of a little cage, wearing a beige prison jumpsuit and orange flip-flops, with hands cuffed. The state did not require the death penalty but a life sentence in prison. Alex Murdaugh wanted to speak. Standing up and looking straight ahead, he repeated what he’d already said: “I am innocent. I never would have hurt my wife, Maggie, and I never would have hurt my son, Paul.”

Before pronouncing the sentence, Judge Newman delivered his assessment of the case, one of the most troubling that he had ever been assigned to preside over. "We have a woman assassinated, a son savagely killed, a lawyer, a person from a respected family who has controlled justice in this community for a century, a person whose grandfather's portrait used to hang at the back of this courtroom." They had crossed paths numerous times in the past, and Newman had trouble understanding how such a sociable and kind being could have ended up in such a situation.

When he announced the sentence, Newman also said this: "I have presided over murder cases for the past twenty-two years. I don't remember a single defendant who was able to recount the moment when he pulled the trigger to kill." He added, "I am sure that Maggie and Paul come to haunt you when you're trying to sleep . . ."

Alex Murdaugh's face was frozen in a funereal mask. His lips parted, and he nodded. "Every day and every night."

"I'm sure of it, and they will continue to do so. And reflect on the last time they looked you in the eyes, as you looked the jury in the eyes."

Did Alex Murdaugh have any final words?

"I will say it again. I respect this court, but I am innocent. I would never have hurt my wife, Maggie, under any circumstances, and I would never have hurt my son, Paw-Paw, under any circumstances."

"Maybe it wasn't you. Maybe it was the monster that you have become by consuming twenty, forty, fifty, sixty opioid pills. You have become a different person. I have already seen it . . ."

For the murders of his wife and son, the judge sentenced Alex Murdaugh to prison "for the rest of your natural life."

Many questions remained unanswered.

First: Exactly what happened on the evening of June 7, 2021? Did Alex Murdaugh just lose it? Or had he been planning the murders for a long time? Why did he kill Maggie and Paul but not Buster? Would we ever know the truth? That is not likely. Murdaugh is the only one who knows, but he lies every time he opens his mouth.

Second: Where did the money go? About $2.5 million went through his dealer, Curtis "Eddie" Smith, who was in contact with traffickers. During the trial, Alex Murdaugh confirmed consuming $50,000 worth of oxycodone per week, which is impossible. What did he do with the money that he didn't spend on pills?

Did he squander it all? Or did he have a fortune hidden somewhere?

Third: Was Alex Murdaugh a black sheep, or was he the exaggerated example of systemic dysfunction? For some, this whole story was linked to the rampant, gangrenous corruption in South Carolina, the good ol' boy system, and the separation of powers established after the Civil War. Bill Nettles, who was US attorney for the district of South Carolina under President Obama, sees things differently. "People try to make this into the whole history of the South," he analyzed. "But that is not the case. It's just human nature, man."

14

THE REST OF HIS NATURAL LIFE

It was 6:30 p.m. on March 3, 2023, and sunlight was warming Walterboro. In front of the courthouse, journalists and the technicians were hugging one another, high-fiving and exclaiming, "Proud of you!" They were packing up: folding up tripods, tents, and camp chairs; pulling carts; filling car trunks; and pulling up cables buried under the ground like roots. In stocking feet and standing on a towel, a news anchor had pulled off her high heels for her last on-the-spot reporting.

Bags of equipment lay on the green grass. The rumble of generators was winding down. His white hair combed back, Scott Grooms, the Walterboro director of tourism, was inviting everyone to come back in April for the Rice

Festival—but the exhaustion evident on his face really seemed to be saying, "Go away."

The food trucks set sail. Then, one after another, the trucks with antennae left the parking lot and headed off. Under a vast pink sky, the circus was leaving town. Full steam ahead for Idaho. There, another case was attracting the attention of Americans: a doctoral student in criminology who was suspected of killing four students.

The hurricane left behind a strange froth that was simultaneously murky, bitter, and joyous. Townspeople exchanged the best moments of the trial like lines from their favorite TV shows. One fan knitted dolls based on her favorite characters from the trial.

At home, in front of his television, Terry McLeod, a resident who had followed the whole trial on live stream, laughed at a joke about the Alex Murdaugh trial on *Saturday Night Live*. Becky Hill, the court clerk, flew off to New York, where the jurors had been invited to do a media tour. She would soon come out with a book, a behind-the-scenes story of the trial. Judge Newman took photos with his fans. In front of Theresa's store, Jim Griffin stuck his face through a hole in the sign to look like a cowboy riding a giant chicken. "I was at the Murdaugh trial."

Spring had come early; the wisteria and azaleas were already in bloom. Life began to slow down. The streets of Walterboro were calm, like the day after a carnival, as if it had all just been a bad dream. The Wildlife Center was deserted, the voices narrating the pedagogical videos on reptiles echoing in the empty rooms. Scott Grooms was busy paying bills. A Fox News journalist was wandering around, wondering what there was left to tell. Then nothing.

In his office with plush carpeting, Mayor Bill Young wondered what day it was. On the whole, he was satisfied with how the past weeks had gone, as everyone had been on their best behavior. He had mixed feelings. "It's both a relief and a letdown," he explained. On the one hand, Walterboro was on the map. On the other hand, the circus had left its mark, and they had felt the glare of the evil eye. Now, people would need to be given the desire to make a comeback in the slow season, beyond the murder trials. How could he turn the situation to the town's advantage? The question would surely come up at the next municipal council meeting. For the time being, it was too soon to draw conclusions about the economic impact, estimate the flow of tourism long term, and decide if, in the end, this case had been good or bad for the region.

A new day was dawning on Hampton. Until that point, the county had known only Murdaughs. Sitting on his front porch across from the courthouse, Sam Crews III, a historian, was going through his mail. He had known the old Buster, Randolph III, Alex, the whole family, and the whole history of Hampton County. Recently, he'd been on Netflix, talking about it. A few days after the end of the trial, he was nervous, even more than usual. His voice was louder, his face a little redder.

After the broadcast of a three-part documentary, he'd received messages. Good ones and not-so-good ones. A video was also posted on Twitter, and his past had come back to haunt him. A lawyer in Columbia with five hundred thousand subscribers was outraged: What was Samuel Francis Crews III doing on Netflix? For years before becoming a teacher and a historian, he had been a lawyer. And he'd been disbarred for embezzlement in 2010. "People disappoint me," said Sam Crews III. "Everyone tries to get people to talk about them on the internet . . ." To take his mind off it, he suggested we take a tour of the cemetery of Hampton. Randolph Murdaugh III's tombstone had been set in place the day after the verdict, like a symbol.

A woman with a dog on a leash was standing near the graves of Maggie and Paul. Sam Crews approached and, recognizing her, said, "Hello, my dear, how are you?" It was Lynn, the sister of Alex Murdaugh. She smiled. For a moment, they held each other in a hug. Sam Crews gave her the items he'd picked up off the grave of Randolph III. A fishhook, a golf ball, and a rifle cartridge. They talked about the trial, the past, and the good that had been destroyed by this story.

A car drove up. A couple of tourists got out and walked over to them. "Could you do me a favor?" Sam Crews whispered to them. "This woman is part of the family . . . could you come back a little later?" They were so sorry; they didn't know. Since the documentary had been broadcast on Netflix, the curiosity seekers had been making their way to the cemetery—about a hundred of them each day. A second car appeared with another couple on board. "It's ridiculous," said Lynn with pain in her voice and left the area in tears. Another car pulled up.

One case remained unsolved. What had happened to Stephen Smith, the young man found on the side of the road in 2015? A week after the trial ended, his mother, Sandy, met me at a Mexican restaurant a few yards from the law firm where the name Murdaugh had disappeared from the sign. She ordered a margarita with sugar on the rim. Fine lines ran across her gentle face, and her eyes lit up at the mention of her son and his dimple, his sweetness, the age that he would be today. In a low voice, she said simply—for there were not a hundred ways to express the pain she had to live with—"He was just my boy."

On the subject of the case, she had already told all that she knew and was trying hard to understand why journalists continued to call on her. Recently, it was Court TV and the *New York Post.* She had said yes to HBO but no to Netflix. "They wanted to buy my son's story, but it is not for sale." During the trial, she stayed away. "It was already enough of a circus, as it was." She thought that justice had been done for Maggie and Paul but took no joy from that. "It's just sad," she said. Now that the Moselle murders had been adjudicated, she was looking for other answers.

In the wake of the murder of Maggie and Paul, the police reopened their investigation into the death of her son, Stephen. For Sandy Smith, this meant a glimmer of hope, but she remained cautious. After eight years of fighting for the truth, she had come to expect disappointment and disillusionment. On social media, she avoided reading the latest theories and rumors, even if she still ended up hearing about them. "The amateur detectives do more harm than good" was her judgment. Several times, she repeated, "Nobody is very capable of compassion."

On March 21, 2023, the police reclassified the death of Stephen Smith as a homicide. When she heard the news, Sandy felt something akin to peace. In early April, her son's body was exhumed for a second autopsy. At the time of this writing, the same lawyers, experts, and journalists are pursuing this investigation. And if they move away from the Murdaugh trail in the end, it doesn't matter. Sandy Smith just wants to know the truth.

"Buster's next!" shouted some crazed person when Alex Murdaugh was taken away to prison for the rest of his life.

Since 2015, the name of the older son kept coming into the case. In March 2023, the twenty-six-year-old had commented for the first time through his lawyer, Jim Griffin. "I have done my best to ignore the vicious rumors implicating me in the tragic death of Stephen Smith, and which continued to be published in the media, while I was mourning the barbarous murders of my mother and my brother. My thoughts are with Stephen's family."

The rumor is tenacious and is anchored in the minds of those who have a fascination for the Murdaughs. Photographers hounded Buster, a mysterious car started parking outside his house, an SUV tailed him. He was being tracked like an animal and was destined to provide fuel for a soap opera that could never fully satisfy America. Whatever the truth was, the young man had understood one thing: for a long time, being a Murdaugh was a privilege, but now it had become a curse he would have to endure.

At the Colleton County Courthouse, the hearing room is deserted, and the lights are turned off. The portrait of old Buster Murdaugh is hanging on its nail again. In the darkness, his pale face radiates calm. His gaze serene and holding a long cigar in his relaxed hand, he keeps watch over this land of pines and swamps that people call the Lowcountry.

APPENDICES

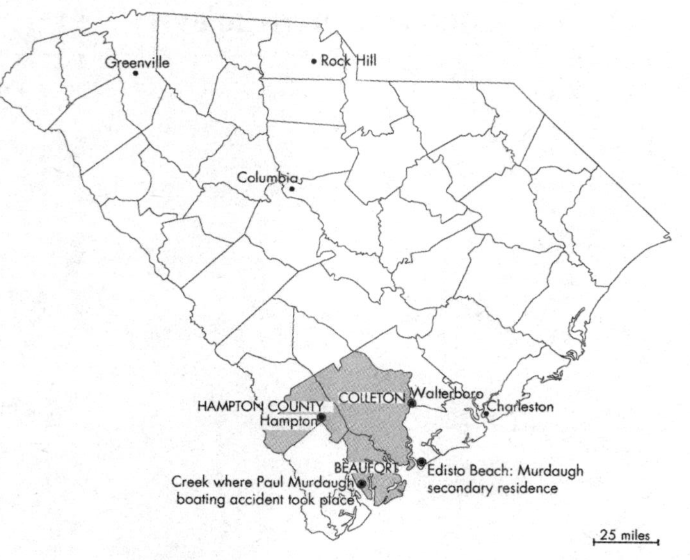

MAP OF SOUTH CAROLINA

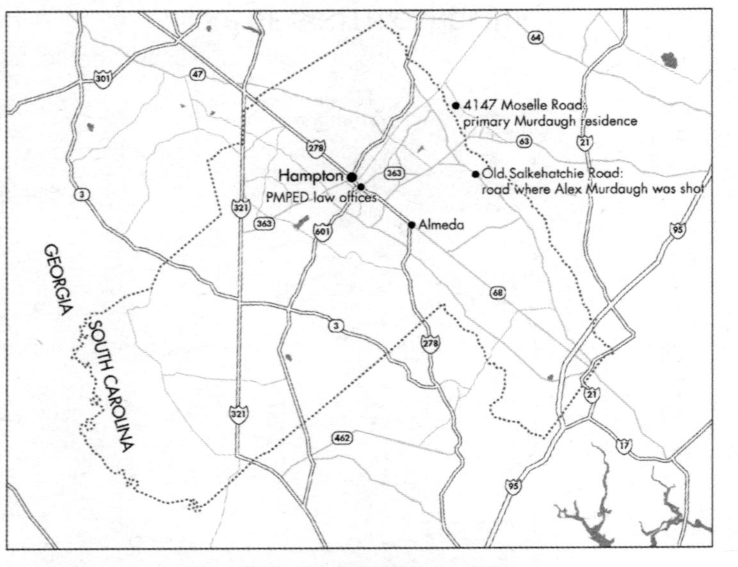

MAP OF HAMPTON COUNTY

Timeline

1885: The Murdaugh family moves to Hampton.

July 19, 1940: Randolph Sr., the first solicitor in the family, is hit by a train.

November 15, 1951: A police raid on a bootleg whisky distillery reveals the involvement of several powerful men in the region, including Randolph Murdaugh Jr., in what will be called the "Whisky Conspiracy of Colleton County."

September 17, 1956: The trial for the Whisky Conspiracy of Colleton County begins. Several men will be convicted, but not Randolph Murdaugh Jr., though accused by some of being the brains behind the operation.

1986: Randolph Jr. is forced to retire after forty-eight years of service. His son, Randolph III, will succeed him.

February 5, 1998: South Carolina mourns the death of the legendary Randolph Murdaugh Jr.

July 8, 2015: The body of Stephen Smith, an openly gay student, is found. Smith had confirmed being involved with an influential man of Hampton County. The name Murdaugh comes up in several areas of the investigation.

February 2, 2018: Gloria Satterfield, the housekeeper at the Murdaugh residence for over twenty years, suffers a fall on the steps leading up to the front door of the residence. She dies three weeks later of her injuries. The circumstances of her fall are murky.

February 2019: Aboard a boat belonging to his family, Paul Murdaugh collides with a bridge piling with five of his friends who are also on board. One of them, Mallory Beach, nineteen years old, loses her life in the accident. Paul is charged with several crimes.

June 7, 2021: Maggie Murdaugh and her son Paul Murdaugh are shot dead at their residence on Moselle Road.

June 22, 2021: The investigation into the death of Stephen Smith is reopened.

August 11, 2021: The first interrogation of Alex Murdaugh takes place.

September 4, 2021: Alex Murdaugh calls the police and declares that an unknown person tried to shoot him while he was changing a flat tire on his car.

October 14, 2021: Alex Murdaugh is arrested for embezzling money that was due to Gloria Satterfield's children.

July 14, 2022: Alex Murdaugh is interrogated by Agent David Owen, who informs him that he is suspected of the murders of his wife and his son.

January 23, 2023: The Murdaugh trial begins and will last twenty-eight days. More than seventy witnesses will testify.

March 2, 2023: The verdict is rendered by the jury: Alex Murdaugh is declared guilty of all charges and will be condemned to a sentence of life in prison.

Murdaugh Family Tree

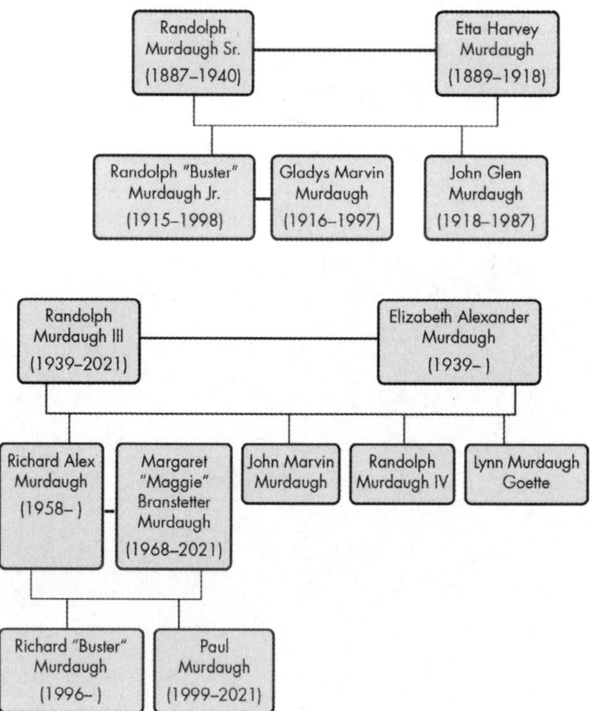

Sources

This book was possible thanks to my six-week attendance at the Alex Murdaugh trial at the Colleton County Courthouse and some thirty interviews between Hampton, Columbia, and Walterboro.

This story never could have been told without the work of the local journalists who had been following the case for years, especially Michael DeWitt, John Monk, Will Folks, Mandy Matney, Liz Farrell, and Brooke Brunson.

The book is based on archival research using the national and local press and the documentaries and podcasts produced on the subject: the *New York Times*, the *New Yorker*, the *New York Post*, the *Daily Mail*, the *State*, the *Post and Courier*, the *Hampton County*

Guardian, the *Murdaugh Murders Podcast*, the HBO documentary *Low Country: The Murdaugh Dynasty*, the Netflix documentary *Murdaugh Murders: A Southern Scandal*, the threads of reviews of reporter Avery Wilks, the *Law & Crime* live stream, archives of the *Post and Courier* at the Charleston Public Library, the *Hampton County Guardian* archives at the Hampton County Public Library, the book titled *Both Sides of the Swamp* (1997), and the book titled *From the Salkehatchie to the Savannah* (2006).

Acknowledgments

Terry McLeod, Becky Hill, Scott Grooms, John Monk, Joe McCulloch, Will Folks, Michael DeWitt, Jason Ryan, Bill Nettles, Kim Brant, Sam Crews III, Brooke Brunson, Andrew Davis, Jamie Harrelson, Trey Harrelson, Janice Harrelson, Bill Young, Amy Scheer, James Tuten, Eric Bland, Sandy Smith, Polly, Alex Postic, Suzanne Andrews, Thad Moore, Ted Clifford, Edgar Castillo, the team at Coconut's, the residents of Walterboro, Stéphane Régy, and Elsa Delachair.

About the Author

Arthur Cerf has been a journalist for *Society* magazine since 2015 and for *Vanity Fair* since 2020. He writes articles on a wide variety of subjects, such as a criminal affair involving Freemasons, false spies, business coaches; a personal development guru; the hyperloop race; a fallen start of French Tech; the creator of Chatroulette; a race between a man and a horse; and young people who are looking for happiness in the country.